T0356174

NOT
GOOD
ENOUGH
GIRL

NOT GOOD ENOUGH GIRL

A Memoir of an Inconvenient Daughter

SONDRA R. BROOKS

SHE WRITES PRESS

Copyright © 2025 Sondra R. Brooks

All rights reserved. No part of this publication may be reproduced, distributed, or transmitted in any form or by any means, including photocopying, recording, digital scanning, or other electronic or mechanical methods, without the prior written permission of the publisher, except in the case of brief quotations embodied in critical reviews and certain other noncommercial uses permitted by copyright law. For permission requests, please address She Writes Press.

Published 2025

Printed in the United States of America

Print ISBN: 978-1-64742-766-5
E-ISBN: 978-1-64742-767-2
Library of Congress Control Number: 2024918849

For information, address:
She Writes Press
1569 Solano Ave #546
Berkeley, CA 94707

Interior design and typeset by Katherine Lloyd, The DESK

She Writes Press is a division of SparkPoint Studio, LLC.

Company and/or product names that are trade names, logos, trademarks, and/or registered trademarks of third parties are the property of their respective owners and are used in this book for purposes of identification and information only under the Fair Use Doctrine.

NO AI TRAINING: Without in any way limiting the author's [and publisher's] exclusive rights under copyright, any use of this publication to "train" generative artificial intelligence (AI) technologies to generate text is expressly prohibited. The author reserves all rights to license uses of this work for generative AI training and development of machine learning language models.

Names and identifying characteristics have been changed to protect the privacy of certain individuals.

To Wonderhubby

Without your help and encouragement, this book could not exist. The endless errands and chores you took care of gave me the time and space to write. You're a true partner in life, and I would marry you all over again.

And to Spud, Highway, Morticia, Belle, Beanie, Yoda, Little Black Dog, Fast Eddie, Sammy, Pita, Rodie, Miss Cabochon, and Puggy Sue. Though some of you are no longer with us, know that your paw prints are all over this book. Thank you for letting me be your mom.

This book is a memoir.

It reflects my present recollections of experiences over time. Some names and characteristics have been changed, some events have been compressed, and some dialogue has been re-created.

I did my best to write a truthful story, and I acknowledge that others' memories of events may differ. I did not write this book to cause harm but to process and better understand the story of my life. May my understanding, such that it is, somehow help others better process their own stories.

Many a reader may find some of the events herein so odd as to be thought contrived, and many actions (my own included) as too dysfunctional to be real. But mine is a family that may have achieved a rare distinction by the sheer number of our spectacular faults.

As they say, "You can't make this stuff up."

PART I

Chapter One

"What kind of daughter does such a thing?" Mom wailed.

I stood in the kitchen with the phone held away from my ear. Never had I heard my mother shriek, not at anyone or anything. I put the phone close to my ear again, ready to deliver a defensive reply, but she continued.

"I've tried to make a life here. Now everyone in town is going to know my daughter hates me!"

"I don't hate you."

"Yes, you do. Any daughter who writes such things about her mother *has* to hate her. She *has* to."

"Mom, I really don't think I—"

"Even my attorney and priest looked at it and asked, 'What is this thing? What is it? What has your daughter done?'"

I could only hope her intense anger might exhaust her a little. I didn't have the courage to hang up on her. I didn't trust my ability to come from a position of strength. I was in my fifties but still afraid to fully test the I'm-a-separate-person-from-my-mother muscle.

"This could destroy my court case! I guarantee you, it's going to be used as part of my character assassination," she said.

"You think their attorneys read my blog? You think people are automatically found guilty based on blog posts someone writes about them? Jesus, we'd all be in jail," I said.

"Oh, listen to you, talking like *you're* a lawyer or something."

I sighed.

"I have to go," she said. "I have an appointment with my priest, who's going to help me decide what to do about this."

"Oh," I said. "Yeah, okay."

"Satan is trying to destroy my marriage!" she said and hung up.

A priest—one who had never even met me—was to decide whether my mother ever spoke to me again. More vexing perhaps was how to defend myself against Satan, who, my mother believed, used me as a pawn to destroy her marriage. I feared that I, as a mere atheist mortal, might be a bit outgunned.

My mother's humiliation and panic were due to her discovery of a blog I started years ago called *My Mother Committed Serial Marriage*. I'd abandoned it after creating only a few posts and all but forgot about its existence.

What kind of daughter does such a thing? My mother's question was a valid one. What kind indeed?

When I was four, I came out of the bedroom I shared with my brother, Greyson, and set off to find Mom. She walked down the hallway toward me, and we met outside the bathroom door. A stocky man with salt-and-pepper hair stood at the sink, the lower half of his face covered in shaving cream. He wore only a sleeveless white ribbed undershirt and boxer shorts. His lack of clothing seemed odd; my father never went around the house barely dressed.

"Mommy, who's that man?" He did not turn to acknowledge me but continued shaving.

"That's your new father. He's come to live with us."

Simple enough. The new man, Dan, sat cross-legged on the floor with me that evening and made quarters appear from behind my ear. Then he'd hold out his closed fists. "Pick one," he said.

I'd point where the quarter surely was, having closely watched his moving hands. He'd open his fist and reveal . . . nothing. "Do it again. Do it again!" I'd squeal.

No matter what choice I made, it was wrong. Choose the left hand, it's the right. Choose the right; no, it was the left. This man was the coolest. No one else in my world had ever found quarters behind my ears. I gave no thought to what might have happened to Dad, who, sadly, lacked this rare talent.

Dad had been a Navy pilot, stationed in England, assigned to fly the radar barrier during the Cold War with Russia. As I understand it, he flew back and forth and back and forth, in case Russia sent spy planes or bombers into Allied airspace. The last time he returned home for a leave, Mom said he spent much of his time seated at the large picture window in the living room of our house, where he stared out onto the street for hours and intermittently let out long, dramatic sighs.

"Honey, what's wrong?" Mom asked.

"Nothing. Nothing."

The next day, he returned to his post in the chair at the front window, watched the world go by, and sighed. And sighed.

"Are you sure there's nothing wrong?" she'd ask.

"I'm fine."

Mom said the staring and sighing went on for days.

When Dad pulled the car into the driveway one evening after they'd returned from a party, she turned to him and asked him point-blank. "Are you seeing someone?"

He confessed to an affair with an English woman named Audrey, whom he'd met while stationed overseas. "I guess it means I don't love you anymore," he said.

Mom felt violently sick to her stomach, and every bit of feeling she had for him disappeared in an instant.

The transition between the two men felt seamless to me. Dan floated into our home as unobtrusively as Dad floated out. Greyson and I visited Dad at his new apartment. It was dark, dank, and depressing, to match the mood that enveloped him. The three of us did little more than sit at the edge of the pool, which was enclosed by brown wooden walls, with a section in the roof cut open to allow sunshine. Design fail. We sat in virtual darkness, dangling our feet into cold, leaf-filled water. Dad had little to say. He had to have known he'd messed up terribly. Audrey was back in England, and here he was, about to be single, losing his wife, home, and children.

When Dad dropped us off after the visit, Greyson stood at the front window of our house and cried as he watched the car drive away. Because we had rarely seen Dad anyway, I did not miss him. Besides, here was an entertaining new man sitting on the floor with me, pretending to pull my nose off and hold it (*it* being his thumb) between his bent index and third fingers. "Give it back!" I yelled. He touched the space above my mouth to return my nose to its rightful place. I reached up to verify that it was indeed back where it belonged. Not only could he do magic tricks, he'd bought a Native American headdress for my brother and a glittery baton for me. Things were looking up in my world.

Dan—my new stepfather—ran a music store in a rather dumpy building near downtown Houston. He did well in the music business in the early sixties, an era in which a home wasn't a home without a piano. And, by god, if there was a piano in a house, someone for sure took lessons.

Not only was my mother an accomplished musician on both the organ and piano, she was drop-dead gorgeous. A man had to be dead from the neck up and the waist down not to notice. Tiny, slender, and busty, with gray eyes and naturally caramel-colored hair, she turned heads. While her divorce from my dad was in process, she'd made a trip to Dan's store to buy sheet music. He struck up a conversation and must have thought he'd hit the motherlode: musical, beautiful, and about to be divorced. He separated from his wife, Patsy, to marry Mom.

Dad met Patsy, perhaps through wanting to commiserate about the divorces, and they started dating. When she was laid up with a stomach flu, he visited, sat down on her bed, and proposed. She marveled that he wanted to marry a vomiting woman in a flannel nightgown. They married six weeks after Dan married Mom.

So, as it turned out, the two couples divorced, switched partners, then married.

And here's some fun to add to the mix: both my father and stepfather were named Dan.

My name is the same as my mother's.

I have issues.

Dan, Mom, Greyson, and I started our new life together in an apartment on the other side of Houston while our house was under construction. Our home life seemed to clip along nicely; I can remember no tension or raised voices between the newlyweds. Surely a match made in heaven.

While they were away on a trip, I cut pictures at random out of magazines, taped them to the wall by my bed, and then subjected our ancient German babysitter—Mrs. Hugly—to a rambling, nonsensical story I'd made up based on the order in which the pictures appeared. "And, see, a plane saw an apple in a car and so a man rode a bicycle. And then, um, there was a dog. So, people ate cereal."

Mrs. Hugly sat on my brother's bed and watched my performance, smiled throughout, and offered what I interpreted as rapt attention.

Mom and Dan returned the next day. He appeared at the door of Greyson's and my bedroom, took one look at the taped-up pictures, and stripped his belt through the loops in one motion. "You'll take the paint right off the walls!"

He grabbed me by the shoulder, twisted me around, and

pushed me against the side of my bed. The pain from the belt was so horrific, it took my brain a few moments to fully register it before I started screaming. Dan then started in on Greyson, although he'd had nothing to do with my art project. Satisfied that he'd hit him enough times, Dan turned back toward me. "Oh, you haven't had enough?" he said, and again went at me with the belt.

Maybe the marriage dynamic suddenly changed while they were out of town, or maybe Mom gave him permission to handle our discipline. Maybe Dan knew she was submissive enough to give him free rein in any regard whatsoever; I never once saw her stand up to him. Whatever the reason, the abrupt shift in the atmosphere at home caused my brother, who had always been sweet and engaging, from then on to spend his time holed up in our room.

Shortly after my first experience with the belt, Dan sat in the living room listening to an album through headphones. The cord, which stretched a foot or so off the ground from his head to the stereo about ten feet away, looked like a good jump rope. I jumped back and forth over it a few times. Then, of course, I caught my toe and yanked the headphones off Dan's head. "Wait for me in your bedroom," he said. When he came in, not a word was spoken. He pulled his belt out of his pant loops, turned me around, and went at my tiny target of a butt. The severity of the lashes always took my breath away and caused a choking sensation, but at the moment when it felt impossible for me to bear more, he delivered two or three more strikes, then stopped. He had an uncanny sense of the point at which I'd been sufficiently subdued.

Chapter Two

When construction was complete on our new house, my grandmother Alma—the builder and architect—saw to it that almost every room was decorated and painted or wallpapered in turquoise or purple. We even had turquoise appliances. Every surface in our kitchen was turquoise. The imitation granite floors throughout the lower level of the house were cream colored with streaks of turquoise. The rocks used to build our floor-to-ceiling fireplace were turquoise and matched the turquoise and purple upholstered furniture that surrounded it. The carpet throughout the living areas was turquoise and purple shag, which we frequently raked to make sure it stood up tall and fluffy.

The master bedroom and bath were not decorated in turquoise and purple, for—in a flash of madcap and zany inspiration, it seemed—Alma chose hot pink. The bedspread material matched the padded headboard—a grandiose, curved creation with an upper point that almost reached the ceiling. The furniture was hot pink and sat on lush, soft-as-cotton beige carpet. The wallpaper in the bathroom was a shiny gold, with a cream-colored, flocked, emblem-type design that reminded me of the Boy Scouts or, come to think of it, the New Orleans Saints football team. An oil painting of a nude in a thick gold frame hung above a hot-pink bench. To its side was the toilet, the only privacy for which was a thick mass of floor-to-ceiling gold beads. All who visited our home were given a full tour, and they raved about the decorating.

I saw no other home like ours among my friends or neighbors. It was the time of bathroom wallpaper with windmills and Dutch girls, black-and-white-checked bedspreads, a few beanbag chairs, the ubiquitous piano, and rather lumpy couches. All were functional in design, and few homes had a deliberate tie-in of decor as ours did. But at least in their homes, you could put your feet on the coffee table and even make a little mess here and there. Not so at Casa Dan, where every place we sat, played, or ate framed us all in a sea of turquoise, always immaculate.

I stepped up onto a park bench, walked across the table, jumped down to the bench on the other side, then to the ground, only to turn around and start over. This went on tirelessly, accompanied by my singing "The Farmer in the Dell."

"Why don't you just light somewhere?" Dan often said, not as a question but a warning.

But not on this particular day. When we got home, he called me over to the organ. "I want to try something," he said. He played a melody, told me the words, and taught me an entire song. We began to work together most nights after dinner, and he was a surprisingly patient teacher.

A few months later, Mom and I were on our way to the Warwick Hotel. I didn't understand any particulars, only that I was to sing "Second Hand Rose"—a song made popular by Barbra Streisand in the movie *Funny Girl*—for an audience.

"Maybe we can find Barbra singing it on the radio," Mom said, fiddling with the dial.

A feeling of awe came over me. To think my mother had the power to will people to appear at the radio station to sing! At six years old, I believed televisions contained people who personally performed for whoever happened to turn on their set, and radios broadcast people who stood at a microphone and sang for anyone tuned in to the station. Barbra didn't appear when summoned that day, but I felt certain Mom hadn't given her enough time to do so before we arrived at the hotel.

No one suggested the possibility of my being nervous. I was particularly tiny, so Dan helped me step up on a chair beside the organ. I looked out on a sea of hundreds of faces and began to perform as if it were the most natural thing in the world.

My repertoire soon increased to include "You'll Have to Put a Nightie on Aphrodite," "Ma, He's Making Eyes at Me," and "Baby Face." Before I sang the latter two, Dan always rose from the organ bench and turned to address the audience. "And now I need a volunteer. How about you, sir?" he'd indicate with an outstretched hand. "Will you step up here and stand by my daughter?"

When I sang that the man had "the cutest little baby face," I stroked him under the chin as Dan had instructed. It never failed to bring laughter from the audience.

Dan determined my future career to be in the performing arts and appointed himself as my agent. He signed me up for piano and music theory lessons. I started twice-weekly ballet lessons, which could continue, he said, unless my calves got too big. I joined our church children's choir, which rehearsed on Wednesdays after school. Dan required us to attend Sunday worship as a family. If he and Mom had a party on Saturday night, however, chances were good we were off the hook for church because they slept too late for us to make it on time. Dan's devotion usually didn't last more than a few consecutive weeks. We didn't attend for a while, then we did, until he lost interest again. But churchgoing provided good advertising for his music business. So did I.

He mailed letters to Optimist, Rotary, and other service-oriented clubs throughout Houston, asking if they were interested in allowing the two of us to entertain at their lunch meetings. A surprising number responded positively. I left school often to sing, and Dan always introduced me as his daughter. "When you're with me, your last name is the same as mine," he ordered. "Got it?"

When I was a toddler, Mom had started calling me Sissy because my brother couldn't pronounce my name, and I became known as Sissy to almost everyone in our family. "Cissie makes a cuter stage name, so I've changed the spelling," Dan said. At school, I was allowed to use my legal given name. It was my responsibility to know which name I was allowed to use and when.

Mom dedicated her afternoons to shuttling me back and forth all over Houston after school. It was a formidable schedule to maintain: after-school activities four days a week, rehearsals scattered throughout, numerous competitions, plus the occasional Sunday choir performance. After lessons, however, I often waited at least an hour for her to pick me up, and there was hell to pay if I wandered around to pass the time and did not remain in place, ready for her arrival. The wait for Mom could be so long, the buildings where I'd had a lesson or rehearsal were often already locked up for the night. I was too scared to hide behind bushes or in the shadows, so I waited on the sidewalk, trying to make out the shape of her Cadillac. She slowed down, stopped at the curb, and blocked traffic if she had to. I climbed in quickly, and we never said a word about why she was late.

Saturday mornings were spent with Mom at the hair salon where, once a week, she booked a shampoo, style, and manicure. When not running around cleaning something, spinning myself dizzy round and round on the styling chairs, or organizing the stylists' supply trays, I read women's magazines. A woman wrote in one article about having a yeast infection so annoying, she sneaked into the bathroom at a party to have a good scratch.

Another woman felt so lonely without a man, she forced a puppy to sleep pressed up against her chest all night. A woman wrote of being sentenced to jail and recounted the humiliating cavity search. Generally, however, we readers learned ways to keep men happy, one recommendation being the application of a cheerful color of lipstick, plus perfume sprayed about the shoulders before preparing his breakfast. By gosh, we were told, it was the least a woman could do for her husband.

There were advice columns such as "Can This Marriage Be Saved?" The responding psychologist almost always answered in the negative, but I found it difficult to discern what the couples were so worked up about in the first place.

At home, I scanned through Dan's *Playboy* magazines. One of the centerfolds said she loved puppies and peppermint ice cream. *Me too!*

For a while, it seemed Dan ignored Greyson, who avoided full detection by riding his bike, playing at the bayou, remaining silent at the dinner table, or staying in his room reading science fiction. Around the time Greyson was in second grade, Dan implemented the requirement that he bring a certain spiral notebook to school so his teachers could note any incidents of misbehavior. Dan reviewed the comments when he came home from work at night. If the teachers reported nothing, Dan placed a star on a poster-board calendar maintained in the upstairs office. If a teacher listed any infractions, such as speaking without raising his hand or getting up to go to the bathroom without permission, Greyson got the belt. He never told his teachers the result of their daily notations, and they were generous with their entries. Some even expressed what a joy it was to see a parent taking such an active role in their child's education.

It's difficult to fathom the fear that accompanied him every day at school and the anticipation of the nightly performance review. One morning, some classmates grabbed the notebook and ran away with it. He was beside himself with worry, as a story about a stolen notebook was surely an obvious ploy to avoid the belt. It might have even brought greater punishment for "allowing" it to be stolen. Greyson somehow got it back from the boys.

During Greyson's beatings, I hid on the floor between my bed and the wall, hoping to muffle the sound of the wails and the crack of the belt as it hit his skin. He then sat at the dinner table with swollen eyes and a puffy face, but no one paid this any mind.

School, for me, was the safest place in the world. We lived in one of the best districts in the area, and the classrooms were bright and clean. All the teachers knew me, which was at times a double-edged sword. I sang on the PA system, occasionally sang at PTA meetings, and led our class in the morning Pledge of Allegiance and the national anthem. I continued to leave school a few times a month to perform at local service clubs with Dan.

However, Miss Moore—my third-grade math teacher— made one hour of my otherwise happy school day pure misery. Midmorning every day, I left my homeroom class with Mrs. Phillips and walked across the hall for daily humiliation. Miss Moore made me sit in the front row, slightly off to her side, for no other reason I could discern but better accessibility for torment. After we graded our homework each day, the dreaded countdown started. "Raise your hand if you missed zero to three."

Carole—perfect, smug little Carole—always raised her hand. I'd already decided I hated her, ever since she'd mocked me in first grade for failing a math test.

"Raise your hand if you missed four to six." Rarely had this category applied to me. I waited with dread. Miss Moore then unfailingly turned her attention to me, with a preemptive expression of disgust. "Raise your hand if you missed more than six."

Well, you could count on me. My performance bordered on

pathetic, especially since we were rarely assigned more than ten math problems.

One morning, I covered my workbook page with my left arm and raised my right hand to respond to missing far fewer than I had. My lie suggested I'd somehow become a mathematical savant overnight. Miss Moore looked down at the sea of red exes my skinny forearm could not possibly cover. "Get your hands away from that paper! How many did you miss?"

I whimpered an embarrassingly high number, somewhere around nine.

"Get out in the hall! I don't keep liars in my class!"

So, I waited out the rest of the hour in the hallway and had to answer to other teachers passing by as to why I wasn't in class. "I lied about my math."

Miss Moore came out to the hall and ordered me back into her classroom. She took to calling me "Miss Queen Bee" when she addressed me. It didn't help my plight the day I pointed out her spelling error, regarding the upcoming school dinner, on the blackboard. "It says spa-ha-getti," I said, emphasizing the second syllable.

"What?"

"That's not spaghetti. It says spahagetti," I said, pointing at the blackboard.

"No, it doesn't," she said.

I couldn't do math, but I knew how to spell spaghetti. It was my duty—my very obligation—to inform Miss Moore of her error. This was a bad idea.

One morning when Mom arrived late to pick me up to perform, we ran past Miss Moore's classroom on our way to the car. She pulled me aside the next day and leaned over with an expression of deep concern. "I saw you and your mother running down the hall yesterday. Is everything okay?"

"We were late."

"Did you have an emergency?"

"No, I was late to go sing."

It was as if a curtain went down over her eyes. The poor woman had wasted sympathy, the supply of which in my Miss Moore account was already in the negative. She straightened her back and stood over me with what always felt like towering height, and her expression hardened. She had a way of looking at me as if homing in on prey through the scope of a rifle. "What's more important to you, singing or school?"

I knew she had me. She knew she had me. "School," I lied.

She smiled with satisfaction. "Because I can make it so you *never* leave this school to sing."

That evening, I told Dan what she'd said.

"Well, maybe she's right. I won't take you out of school anymore to perform," he said.

This was not only disappointing but confusing, as I'd never seen him roll over for anyone. He didn't, of course, explain his reasoning to me, but from then on, we only performed together at night or on the weekends.

Dan didn't want me to reach adolescence viewing alcohol as something to be experimented with behind his back, so he offered me tastes of the drinks he concocted at his home bar. What elementary school child could resist crème de cacao in ice cream or something as fascinating as a minty green Grasshopper? Or the beautiful gold color and sweetness in the tall and ornate glass bottle of Galliano? Whenever he and Mom entertained, which was almost every weekend, he served alcohol to the guests and always allowed me a taste.

It was the sixties. Dan prepared drinks for the road, and off we'd go to a restaurant with a couple they'd invited for an evening out. Why I so often accompanied them was beyond me, and Dan and

Mom's friends probably couldn't figure out why either. My silence was required during these dinners, and, aside from giving my order to the waiter, I remained mute for hours as the adults talked.

I sat in the front seat between Dan and Mom one evening as five of us rode down Westheimer Road on the way to a restaurant. I took Mom's martini out of her hand and sipped it, finding it shockingly foul tasting. She laughed at my expression, so I took the glass from her again and downed the entire drink. "You're not going to believe what she just did!" Mom said to the couple in the back seat. But she wasn't angry, and the laughter felt good. By the time we got to the restaurant, I had passed out. They left me in the car to sleep it off while they ate dinner.

That same year, Dan enlisted my Aunt Lu to introduce me to cigarettes. Lu was my only aunt, and a glamorous one at that. A former Kilgore Rangerette—a Texas college performing group of young women known for their insanely high kicks—she was a blonde, green-eyed bombshell in her youth. She was beautiful and theatrical, although her voice often sounded a bit whiny.

"Say it like this," she instructed. "Peetah, Peetah, Peetah, I've come for my lettahs. Peetah, you're being an absolute beast, and if there's one thing I can't stand, it's a son of a . . . Peetah, the biscuits are burning!" She provided my acting lesson with an exaggerated strut across the room, one hand on her hip, the other hand waving a lit cigarette back and forth like Bette Davis. "When people ask what you want to do when you grow up, tell them you want to be in the *theatuh*."

Another lesson involved how to handle men. "When you grow up and a man you can't stand wants to marry you, you just cook him a meal that would choke a horse, okay?"

"You've done that?" I asked, wondering why she couldn't just tell a guy to amscray like we did in elementary school.

"Oh, sure. Lots of times," she said. "A man doesn't want to marry a woman who can't cook."

She'd recently been married, but technically only for about an hour, to a man named Charles, whose face could well represent that of an oyster, should an oyster need that sort of visual representation. While his small skull was in keeping with his small build, his forehead jutted so far out, it provided a bony cliff over the lower part of his face. I can't remember him speaking much, and certainly not to me, but each time he came to our home, he ended up singing "On a Clear Day (You Can See Forever)." What he lacked in pitch, he made up for in volume. I'd never known it was physically possible for a human being to sing so loudly.

After their wedding, Charles and Lu decided to stop off at a Houston hospital to share their marital bliss with a sick friend. Charles parked the car, then turned to her. "I've never loved you," he said. "And I never will."

Well, that was that.

So, Lu had some man-free time on her hands, and she appeared more often at our home. During one of her visits, Dan asked her to teach me how to smoke a cigarette. Like the frequent offerings of alcohol, letting me smoke was part of Dan's plan to remove the attraction to vices before my teen years hit.

Mom, Dan, Aunt Lu, and I sat at the circular turquoise-flecked marble table in our turquoise dining room. Lu removed a cigarette from her pack, lit it, and handed it to me. Her hot-pink lipstick prints on the filter made what I was about to do feel all the more cool. She lit one for herself and used it for instruction. "Draw in the smoke like this, breathe through your nose, then blow the smoke out your mouth."

It wasn't a true inhale, so I didn't cough much. The smooth feel of the cigarette between my fingers and the smell of its wafting smoke represented a yearned-for step toward adulthood. Most adults smoked back then, although Dan and Mom, surprisingly, did not. The process of smoking a full cigarette was fascinating, made even more so by doing something so blatantly frowned upon for a child without the fear of being caught or punished. Now I could be as glamorous as Aunt Lu. "Could I have another one?" I asked her.

Lu looked at Dan, whose eyes widened. Dan looked at Mom, who flinched. Dan looked back at Lu. "Okay," he said, shrugging.

The next day, convinced I'd achieved a level of coolness most eleven-year-olds could only dream of, I not only started sneaking cigarettes in the ravine of the bayou behind our house but regularly recruited girlfriends to join me. When Dan found a pack of Salem Menthols in my purse a few months later, he didn't spank me but made me light up, then blow each exhale through a white handkerchief. "See that stuff on the cloth? That's what's going in your lungs."

He never said another word about my smoking. It would be thirty-five years before I stopped for good.

When I was ten years old, I stole Mom's bedside copy of *Everything You Always Wanted to Know About Sex (But Were Afraid to Ask)* and read it cover to cover. Dan somehow found out, told me to write down any questions, and promised to answer them. A few days later I was back, seated on the hot-pink love seat in their bathroom, under an oil painting of a nude woman, who, coincidentally, was also on a love seat. Dan stood in front of me and waited as I referred to my list.

"Where do people do this stuff?" I asked.

"People usually have sex in bed. Usually lying down."

"Why?"

"Why what?" he asked.

"Why do they want to do it?"

Mom's back was to me, her image visible in the mirror where, each morning, she went through the twenty-minute process of teasing, placing, pinning, and spraying her French-twisted hair.

As she listened, she attempted to adjust the height of the puffiness with a pick. She had a slight smile on her face.

"Well, it's something a man and a woman who love each other want to do," he said.

"What's a prophylactic?" I asked, sounding it out phonetically.

"A prophylactic is something the man wears during sex. A woman usually wears something too."

This confounded me for the longest time. How could women wear prophylactics in their vaginas? It took years to figure out that he meant a diaphragm, not a condom.

He was surprisingly cool about my sex education, believing it shouldn't be portrayed as something shameful. He advised that sex was a special, personal sort of thing, and it was best that I not throw this information around at school.

The next day, out on the playground with my friend JoEllen, I felt compelled to educate her. "People usually do it in bed," I sagely informed her after a short lecture. She was not impressed and was in fact surprisingly uninterested, so I spoke no more about it.

Dinner was the time when Dan held court, and he controlled the discussion and the tone of meals. There was little cross talk between family members. The rules changed here and there, but he always required us to ask permission to be excused from the table. One night I forgot. "Get back to the table and sit down," Dan said. I returned to my chair. "Ask permission to be excused." I sat, silent. "You're going to sit there for as long as it takes," he said.

I wanted for once to best him, to outsmart him, to win at any little something, even if it meant sitting there all night. Dan then puttered around in the kitchen, the one room in our house where he spent the least amount of time. He didn't do any women's work, nor, for that matter, any manual labor. But the kitchen gave him the advantage of viewing the dining table and my pending decision. He didn't go upstairs to watch television as he normally did, and his monitoring of me held a sure warning. He, too, could hold his ground all night should I sit there for hours. But the option was ludicrous; he never allowed one of his children to toy with him in any way. My determination caved within minutes.

"May I please be excused?" I asked.

"Yes, you're excused."

One rule was inviolable in our home. We were to say, "Yes, sir" or "No, sir" to any question. I tried to get around this once by saying, "I think so" in response to a question he asked, but Dan was on to me. It seemed downright supernatural how he saw through any attempt to circumvent his rules. As he saw it, a child either knew something or they didn't. "I don't know" or "I'm not sure" wasn't going to fly. He saw the world in black or white—when it wasn't turquoise—and this was especially true when dealing with my brother, for whom quality of life revolved around the number of daily notations in a spiral notebook. Greyson lived in constant fear of inevitable punishment, endured horrific pain, and lived with ongoing emotional damage. He had only a few days a month, mostly on weekends, during which he could simply be a little boy. And yet, Dan never once took a belt to one of us with Mom as a witness, nor did he ever hit us in public. Whichever one of us had misbehaved spent the rest of the day knowing what awaited when we got home. Within minutes of arriving back at the house, he was ready with a belt. He never forgot. He never changed his mind. I assumed that however he treated me, it was how my friends' fathers treated them. He said he loved me; therefore, his actions where I was concerned registered within me as justifiable. Neither Dan nor Mom ever apologized or admitted to being at fault. I interpreted this to mean they never were. Appearances. Image. It meant the world to them.

On any workday, he wore silky suits bordering on garish, in colors such as gold or even puce, and when at home, he dressed in slacks, leather loafers, and usually a knit short-sleeved shirt. He gooped his prematurely gray hair with pink Butch wax after every shampoo, combed the top part straight forward, then expertly flipped it up and over to the side, where it remained glued until the next morning. He only relaxed his self-imposed strict dress code when he took us fishing. Khakis, canvas deck shoes, a knit short-sleeved shirt, and no Butch wax on his hair. During the summers, he took us out in the Gulf of Mexico in his boat, the *Sea Sharp*, countless times. The decision to fish on a given weekend seemed spur-of-the-moment, and the only thing keeping us from the straight shot to Galveston on the Gulf Freeway was a detour stop at Kentucky Fried Chicken for a bucket of chicken livers and Original Recipe. We ate the cold chicken out on the boat and threw the bones overboard. Dan filled our empty soda bottles with water and sank them. No doubt the huge, waxy KFC cardboard buckets ended up at the bottom of the ocean as well.

We always went out so far that we could no longer see land. If Dan ever felt alarmed by a situation, he never let us see it, and, in that manner, we felt safe with him. He allowed Greyson and me to sit on the bow of the boat, where we gripped the wraparound metal railing and positioned our legs around one of the welded vertical bars. The spot of choice was at the very front, and we held on for dear life as Dan took the boat up to high speed. He aimed for choppy water, because the bumpier it was, the more my tiny body was lifted into the air, rendered weightless, then slammed down hard over and over, a sensation that kept me screaming with laughter.

More than once, the Coast Guard spotted us, turned to approach, and came alongside. They warned Dan on their speaker, "Pull your children back into the boat, sir. What you're doing is illegal."

"Oh. Sorry, officer."

We climbed back in. Dan waited until their boat was far off in the distance, then allowed us to get back out on front. Sure, we could have been thrown overboard and shredded by the propellers. We were at great risk of becoming shark bait, but Dan said he'd never seen me enjoy anything more than those boat rides. He continued to break the law for me.

We never failed to catch fish. The task of cleaning them fell to whoever wasn't having as much luck pulling them in, and the fillets were already iced and ready for cooking when we called it a day and returned to shore.

"Does it hurt fish to have hooks in them?" I asked Dan.

"Nah, they don't have any feeling in their mouths."

I must have assumed as well that scaling them while they were still alive didn't cause them pain. One eye gazed up at me as I ran the scaler across their skin over and over. Their struggle ended quickly. Their guts nauseated me, especially the cheese-grits-looking eggs in a female. We threw all entrails overboard to attract more fish.

Late one afternoon, spent and sticky from the heat and salt air, we drove to a diner on the Galveston Seawall. It appeared they'd aimed for a certain decor but either lost their design vision along the way or maybe ran out of money. For some odd reason, the overstuffed semicircular red booths faced away from the view of the ocean or were positioned on the oblique, like a Tilt-A-Whirl ride at rest. We walked in with Dan, a small cooler in tow. It was well after lunch and the restaurant was almost empty. He called out to a Black woman in the kitchen, and she came over to the serving window. "We have a big catch here," he said. "I'm wondering if you'll cook them up."

After serving us, she leaned against the counter and watched us eat, a small smile on her face the entire time. Of all the fish I've eaten, hers was, hands down, the best, and Dan surely paid her well for her efforts. The only certainties about Dan were the contradictions. He stole towels and ashtrays from Holiday Inns but never outright cheated someone. He treated us to fishing trips and unforgettable vacations but beat us with belts. He went to church but never mentioned God. I never saw him be cruel to an animal, nor did I ever see him help one. He asked for what he wanted and seemed to always get it, not only from us but from strangers. In public he portrayed calm, confidence, and amiability. His stock answer to how he was doing, how business was going, or how life was treating him was always the same. "Faaaaaaaaaaaantastic," he'd say, his Texan accent making it a four-syllable word. "Couldn't be better. No complaints at all."

Chapter Three

Patsy had custody of Debbie and Jimmy, the two children she'd had with Dan. She then had two more children with Dad, and all four lived with them. The tension in their home reached a boiling point. Dad supported a household of six, resented Jimmy's presence, grieved the loss of Greyson and me, and began to drink heavily. Mom told him Greyson and I would call when we wanted to see him but told us Dad would call when he wanted to see us. We usually only saw him on our birthdays or for a few hours at Christmas. Such visits were always strained, and Patsy did not seem to particularly welcome our presence. Then again, having us visit meant there were six children in her house at one time. It couldn't have helped her frazzled nerves.

Debbie and Jimmy came home from school one afternoon and found packed suitcases on their front porch. Within a few hours, they were seated in our turquoise dining room having dinner with us. Dan finished his meal, put his elbows on the table, and clasped his hands together. "I have an announcement," he said, with a small smile. "Jimmy and Debbie are going to be staying with us."

His tone of voice presented this development as great fun for all. Jimmy sat across from me, his black hair and olive skin in stark contrast to the turquoise high-backed chair framing his face. His eyes searched our expressions as Dan spoke. Debbie looked shell-shocked, along with Mom. Their mouths smiled slightly but their eyes did not.

"Are they staying a few days?" I asked.

"They'll be here longer than that," Dan said.

That sounded like some fun, actually. "Where will they sleep?" I asked.

"You'll be sharing your rooms with them."

That did *not* sound like some fun.

No one mentioned how long the plan had been in the works, or if Patsy or Dad simply snapped one day, called Dan, and said this was how it had to be and it better be that very day. But Debbie and Jimmy immediately attended a new school, so some arrangements surely were made prior to their arrival. Their friends and all that was familiar were forty-five minutes away. New school, new home, new rules. Luggage on the front porch to living in a new home, all within a few hours. They had to have felt transported into a time warp. Dan tried to sound warm and welcoming, but it didn't appear that Debbie and Jimmy even knew him well, and they'd rarely visited our home before moving in.

Mom decided that four children under her roof required full-time live-in help. Other families in the neighborhood planned to hire women from Mexico to do their housekeeping, and Dan asked that our family be included. One of the neighbors picked them up at the border and brought them to their home, where all of us met on the front lawn. Three families stood around the women, appraising them as if they were auction material. "I'll take that one," someone said, breaking the silence.

"Okay, we'll take her then," another said, pointing.

By default, we ended up with Angela, who spoke not a single word of English. In those days, Spanish was a required course in elementary school, giving me the ability, although haltingly, to communicate with her. At the dinner table that night, Dan told me to tell her that the family had decided to call her Angel, not Angela. When I informed her, she furrowed her brow, then nodded. How entitled of us to believe we should deprive the poor woman of her very name. But we didn't after all, and she was our Angela.

Dan turned the screened-in patio on the back of the house into her room. The screens were switched out to glass, so for privacy she changed clothes in a small storage closet by her bed. No air-conditioning or heat. To access her bedroom, she had to pass through Jimmy and Greyson's room. She was given an electric blanket and space heater for the winter. She told me of nights when she couldn't sleep due to the cold, but I never told Dan or Mom. Apparently, not even one of us thought to ask if her living arrangements on the patio were comfortable or how we might better accommodate her.

I adored her and spent most evenings with her while she crocheted and listened to Spanish radio stations. Using countless incorrectly conjugated verbs, I told her everything about my days at school and asked endless questions about her family. I accompanied her to the mall to help her shop, and we ducked into stores when we saw police officers. "*Policia!*" I said with alarm, fearing a demand to see her *papeles de immigración*, which did not exist.

She let me put blue eye shadow and mascara on her. We watched Spanish soaps together on television, and she tried to explain why the characters always cried and yelled at each other. She frequently asked me to dance ballet for her. Angela became my best friend, my confidante, my trusted mother. I dreaded Sundays, when she was gone all day for church, lunch, and a movie with the other women who came to the United States with her. I wanted her home, always, with me.

Dan adopted a mandatory family meeting, implemented when interpersonal glitches—those that couldn't be handled by physical abuse alone—surfaced. We unfailingly met in the huge glass-walled turquoise living room. Debbie made the mistake of swearing in one of these dreaded meetings. Dan leaned forward and slapped her. "Don't you ever swear at me," he said.

"Well, you swear at me!" she said.

"You're right. I do."

She was the only one of us who had the courage to stand up to him, and he usually left her alone. She adopted the Greyson method, always remaining in her room, except for short nightly visits to the dinner table or, although rare, to the television set in the den when she wasn't doing homework, talking on the phone in her room, or writing letters to Patsy. Maybe she felt she had insufficient privacy to unburden herself by phone.

She had placed a sealed envelope on the kitchen counter, where all mail went before one of us took it to the mailbox at the front of the house. Either Dan or Mom opened it and read Debbie's comment to Patsy that slop was fed to us nightly. My mother couldn't have prepared slop if she'd outright tried. The offense earned us a mandatory family meeting in the living room, ostensibly to root out the cause of Debbie's hostility.

Greyson continued to bring the spiral notebook home after school and await his fate with the belt. As tensions continued to rise, more and more dysfunction was blamed on him, whom Dan took to calling "twerp" when he found him more annoying than usual. He made fun of him at the dinner table if he acknowledged him at all. Greyson sat on the other side of Mom, giving Dan full view of him.

"This is how Greyson eats," Dan announced one night. He filled a spoon with dessert, turned his head to the side, and smeared the food down the side of his cheek. When the wax seal on the hall bathroom toilet failed, he accused Greyson of sloppy aim as the cause of the urine-filled water on the floor. Soon, he and Jimmy spent most of their time grounded, spending every afternoon doing homework at the kitchen table. Dan monitored their grades closely but paid no attention to mine.

Jimmy developed a flat affect; Mom interpreted it as hostility. She determined we were running late for church one Sunday, came into the kitchen, and told him to get a move on. He had his back to her as he rushed to finish his breakfast. He motioned with his index finger to please wait. "Just a minute," he said, around a mouthful of cereal. Mom strode over and slapped him on the face from behind. This called for another family meeting, during which Mom accused Jimmy of taking an insolent tone with her.

All four children missed school the day a professional photographer came to our home to shoot a formal sitting of our family. The portrait showed the six of us as clean, well dressed, relaxed, and somehow pulling off the odd naturalness of hanging out in the backyard while wearing our best clothes. Mom was then photographed alone, with a backdrop of blurry trees and muted sunlight. Several months later, she walked through the Galleria shopping mall and saw her image on display. There was a large ribbon attached to the frame in the window of the photography studio. Her portrait had won an award. She looked stunning.

Dan was not the kind of man to admit his home and business life were anything but a raging success. Here was a man who had read all the best-selling books on achievement. He could quote Zig Ziglar and Dale Carnegie and often shared their wisdom with me. He was the proud owner of a wooden coin with "Round Tuit" stamped on it, meaning there was never justification in life by claiming, "I'll do it when I get around to it." The Lifebook of Dan proclaimed, by god, if a person wasn't successful, they needed to get their head out of their ass and try harder. So, if all aspects of Dan's home life weren't buzzing along merrily, well, those little square pegs of annoyance were going to be forced into round holes. Even if it required more of the belt.

Our family drew admiration: a successful businessman, a beautiful and talented wife, a stylish and immaculate home in a desirable neighborhood. And look at those children, so happy and well adjusted. Not a single one in juvenile detention. And that little girl—the one who sings. The apple of her stepfather's eye.

Being Dan's favorite gave me a certain amount of protection. It also became a curse. Either he or Mom came into my bedroom to tuck me in every night, and I waited and watched for whoever appeared. The door remained open due to my fear of the dark. The swishing sound of the dishwasher running through its cycles signaled the end of another day and helped lull me to sleep.

If Mom came in, she kissed my palms, and I turned this into a game of holding her kisses inside my closed fists as long as possible. When Dan came in, he licked his lips and kissed me on the mouth, a habit I hated but could do nothing about. I grew to hate wet kisses on my face as well and wiped off sticky saliva in disgust. The only time I remember my friend JoEllen spending the night, Dan came in to say goodnight, then kissed both of us on the mouth. "JoEllen gave me a little-girl kiss last night, but you gave me the kiss of a woman," he said the following morning.

I'd only seen television and movie kisses, really, and didn't know that I'd done anything differently, much less given the kiss of a woman, but Dan was pleased. After he and Mom came home from an evening out, he took an instamatic camera shot of me sleeping with my gigantic hot-pink stuffed poodle at my side. My face was turned toward the camera, my mouth hung open, and my arms and legs were splayed out toward all corners of the bed. My nightgown had ridden up, exposing much of my underwear. Dan presented the photo to me the next morning. My bedroom light was on when he'd taken the shot, and seeing this stirred a sense of violation I couldn't name or verbalize. Even Angela got to see me splayed out and unconscious, and she pointed one of her long fingernails at my crotch—presented for the camera in white cotton little-girl underwear—and giggled.

One evening, he entered my room to tuck me in. As always, he bent over, kissed me on the mouth, and told me he loved me. But this time, instead of immediately turning around and leaving, he lowered himself on top of me, stretched his legs out between mine, and laid his head on my chest. I stared at the ceiling, unsure of what to do, and waited for him to leave. Then his hands were up under my nightgown, moving toward my chest. He took my nipples between his fingers and squeezed them. The sensation was new and disturbing. Irritating. My body went rigid. I didn't pull away, not only because of his weight pressing me down but because I couldn't tell him to stop.

My nipples felt reduced to the size of pinheads, clamped between his short, stocky fingers. I looked toward the flickers of light and shadow that turned my turquoise-and-purple room into odd shades of gray and black. Someone was in the den, only a few steps away from my bedroom, watching television without volume. I hoped it was Mom. I didn't take my eyes off the door and willed her to please, please, please come help me.

Dan and I lay there together, his head turned to the side and resting on my chest. Perhaps he, too, was watching the door. He wanted something from me that night; I could feel myself fulfilling a need I did not understand. He seemed sad and wanting, gentle and lost.

I don't know how long he remained on top of me. He removed his hands from under my gown, got up, and walked out of the room. He didn't have to warn or threaten me not to tell—I didn't know *how* to tell. I couldn't have explained why I didn't call out for Mom. Or why I lay there and let his touching continue, even though my hands were free, resting on the pillow, on either side of my head. Who would possibly understand why I did not, could not, ask him to stop?

I pedaled up to our house one Saturday and was happy to see Patsy standing in the driveway. I dropped my bike on the grass, called out "hey," and ran over. She paced back and forth like a caged animal alongside her blue Impala. There was a long, dark streak of color on the front of her pale blue dress. "Hey, Patsy. What's up?"

"Seems we're having a bit of trouble this morning," she said.

We? Not me. I'd done nothing more than take a bike ride around the neighborhood.

Mom opened the front door of the house. She sported a teased-up, Phyllis Diller–style hairdo that didn't look good on her at all. I figured she'd already been to the beauty parlor and back, which was odd because she hadn't taken me with her as she always did. "Get in here!" Mom yelled.

Patsy reached into her car and opened the glove compartment. She turned toward me and pointed a pistol at my head. "How 'bout I make a deal with you?" she called out to Mom. "You give me my children and I'll give you yours."

Mom looked as if her legs were going to give out from under her. "Cissie, I mean it! Get in this house!" she yelled.

"Stay where you are," Patsy said, maintaining her aim.

"Get in here! Now!" Mom called out in a ragged voice.

Dan appeared behind her at the doorway and ordered me inside. I took a step toward the house. Patsy flicked the gun back and forth, as if I needed a reminder that it was still there. "Stay," she ordered.

"Cissie, you get in this house, and you do it now," Dan said. He didn't raise his voice—he never had to. And an angry Dan was far scarier than an armed stepmother.

"Sorry, Patsy, but I gotta go," I said. Yes, I apologized. There was a lot of lawn to cover before reaching the front door, and maybe I thought if I was polite, she'd go easy on the number of pops she delivered to the back of my head.

After I ran into the house, Dan ordered me to go upstairs to the master bedroom and wait for him. When he entered, he undid his belt and stripped it through his pant loops. "The next time your mother tells you to do something, you do it."

A few days later, Mom provided the details. Debbie and Jimmy were to spend the remainder of the weekend with Patsy. When she arrived to pick them up, Dan and Jimmy were visible through the glassed-in game room that looked out on the front lawn. Dan delayed in sending Jimmy out until he resolved an issue with his homework. Patsy interpreted the delay as Dan's intention to prevent Jimmy from leaving with her. She strode up the driveway and came into the house. Over six feet tall and made of sturdy country stock, she had no problem delivering a football tackle to my ninety-five-pound mother and throwing her to the floor. She grabbed Mom's hair in her fists, creating the Phyllis Diller hairdo I didn't like, and repeatedly hit her head against the tile. The dark streak I'd seen down the front of Patsy's dress was Mom's blood. Dan wrestled her out of the house, and I'd appeared in the driveway about then, all happy-go-skippy on my bike.

When Patsy arrived back at the home she shared with Dad, did she confess that there had been a bit of a, shall we say, kerfuffle? Whatever she said, it's safe to assume she omitted the part about the gun.

Dan and Mom never argued in front of us but could at times be found in their bedroom engaged in quiet, tense discussions. We saw no reason to believe they were anything but a united front, but Debbie and Jimmy's presence in our home gnawed at Mom.

Dad, as well, had resented them when they'd lived in his home, not only because supporting so many children under his roof was difficult. In addition to providing basic care for Dan's children, he was required to pay Mom $100 a month in child support for Greyson and me, though he never paid a cent. Greyson and I, up to that point, had a permanent home. The children Dad and Patsy had together had a permanent home. Jimmy and Debbie did not, and their presence in our house always felt a bit tenuous, as if not even one of us ever fully regarded them as family.

Debbie graduated from high school and drifted out of our home and into a life that did not include us. Patsy came to pick up Jimmy, and we watched as she loaded his luggage into the trunk of her car. Mom looked relieved. He was sent to Allen Military Academy, from which he went AWOL and was expelled. He moved back into Patsy and Dad's home. The tension in their house continued to grow.

It's uncertain if Dan recognized that everyone in his turquoise-and-purple wonderland exhibited signs of pent-up, simmering anger. My newly disrespectful and hostile attitude at school landed me in the principal's office more than once, and my report cards at the time showed failing grades, even in reading and spelling, two subjects I could have only failed with intention.

One day at my friend Betsy's house across the street, I sneaked into her parents' bedroom and stole a ring from the top of the chest of drawers. Her mother had never been anything but kind to me and even at times showed me warm affection, but I resented the home life Betsy got to have. I held the ring in my fist and spent the remainder of my time in her house with my arms folded across my chest, a demeanor meant to make me look nonchalant. On my way home, I threw the ring into the twenty-foot-high bamboo hedge bordering their driveway. "My mom knows you took her ring," Betsy said the next time I saw her. No one said anything more to me about it. Had Dan been informed and confronted me, I'd have folded like a cheap tent and confessed.

Greyson and a friend vandalized a construction site and caused over $100,000 of damage. If Dan knew, he did nothing. This was not surprising, however, as it wasn't the glaring infractions or outright crimes we may have committed that drove him to physical abuse. He majored in the minor, and the small annoyances in life drove him to distraction, especially in child-rearing. His children were to be obedient, and robotically so. The idea that he might seek our opinion was ludicrous. Feelings didn't matter; doing what he told us to do mattered. Even if we toed the line to the best of our ability, there loomed the risk that we'd err accidentally. We were watchful and vigilant and learned to tune in to the changing moods and energy around us. Our spirits were subdued, and our voices were silenced by the belt.

Only rigid adherence might save us. I began to obsess over my mistakes, ruminating on them for weeks on end. I overthought anything I'd said at school that might have made me look foolish. Embarrassing moments played in my head in an endless loop. After not winning first place in a district talent show, the loss nagged at me for weeks on end. I burst into tears, unable to hold in my shame any longer. "Why didn't I win?" I whined to Dan.

"You were too cocky when you came out onstage."

This was news to me, and the revelation told me there were additional flaws in me, ones only others could see. I began to obsess about these as well. The slightest mistake threw me into days of all-encompassing self-doubt.

Chapter Four

I often developed tonsillitis, resulting in frequent appointments with our new doctor, Vance, a tall olive-skinned man with large, slightly bulbous gray eyes. He'd given me no cause to either like or dislike him; he was just my doctor. His short, helmet-like hair, however, fascinated me; it looked like silver Brillo pads. Dan and Mom became friends with him and his wife, and they often socialized and traveled together. Soon, I went to the doctor much more than usual, and I didn't always know the reason until Mom declared it to Vance when he walked into the exam room. Greyson accompanied me only once. He sat in the back seat of the car, and Mom spoke to him via the rearview mirror. "Greyson, don't tell Dan you went to the doctor today, okay?"

"Why?" he asked.

"Just don't, okay?" I said, turning to look at him. I already knew the rules but couldn't have said, exactly, how I'd learned them. What Mom and I did together on any given day was never discussed with Dan anyway, at least not by me, for what interest could there possibly be in the endless weeks of ballet, piano, drama rehearsals, and choir performances, with the occasional doctor or dentist appointment thrown in?

"What seems to be the problem?" Vance asked.

"I want them tested for worms," Mom said.

He seemed surprised but took the time to explain the symptoms and his belief that it was unlikely we were afflicted. Mom's eyes looked squinty as she listened, and her expression threw a sure and certain heat at him throughout his worm lecture. "But if it will make you feel better, they can be tested," he said. He sent her home with two cardboard cups for our stool samples. I hid the collection cup under my sink, hoping Mom might forget. The cup's presence haunted me every time I entered my bathroom. *Every* time. After weeks of worrying that the requirement for a sample yet loomed—my mind always obsessing on the correct way someone even went about doing this—I finally got the courage to sneak the collection cup into the kitchen, hide it in the bottom of our trash compactor, and crush it into oblivion. Problem solved.

When my tonsillitis returned for perhaps the third time, Vance scheduled a tonsillectomy. He didn't perform the surgery but included me in his hospital rounds. His wife, with whom Mom had become good friends, stopped in to visit as well, and the two women sat and chatted for a few minutes. Dan never visited, although I stayed in the hospital for five days. On the morning of my scheduled release, Mom slipped Vance a piece of paper. He read it, looked at me, and smiled. "On second thought, I think you need to stay another night."

A few weeks later, Mom and I met Vance for lunch after one of my summer ballet lessons. Not knowing beforehand that we were to meet him, I'd brought nothing to wear over my leotard and tights and felt all but naked going through the serving line, which was jam-packed with people. It was a blessed relief to finally sit down and hide my body. Our family had a preference for where we sat at the cafeteria—up front and near a window—but Mom and Vance chose the crowded area, far in the back. They sat across from me, chatting about this and that, and the angle of their arms told me they were holding hands under the table.

Mom was always home at night, unless she and Dan were out with their friends or away on a trip. That night, however, her absence went unexplained. As I lay in bed, I heard Dan rummaging around in the closet at the top of the stairs. There were only two things in that closet: air-conditioning equipment and luggage. "Daddy? What are you doing?" I called out.

"I'm leaving," he said.

"Why are you leaving?"

He came downstairs and appeared as a dark shadow at my bedroom door. "You know who you had lunch with today?" he asked.

"Yes," I said, my voice weak and whiny.

"That's why I'm leaving." He didn't come in to say goodbye or give me a wet kiss on the mouth. I listened to his footsteps going back and forth above me in the master bedroom as he packed. He came downstairs again, then was gone.

Mom and I had been followed by a private detective. The marriage was over.

PART II

Chapter Five

Dan moved out permanently and filed for divorce. He also filed an Alienation of Affection suit against Vance and obtained a restraining order. Not only did Dan wish to complicate their access to one another, but he threw as many legal headaches at Vance as possible. But it seemed nothing could keep the two of them apart.

After picking me up from a ballet lesson one evening, Mom drove down the street from the studio to a nearby drive-in theater and, without explanation, pulled into the lot and parked. Vance ran toward us, and he and Mom got into the back seat of our car. I watched a silent movie, not knowing how to operate the dials on the pole by the window. Something about a car speeding through San Francisco. Police chase scenes. Bad guys with evil expressions. A criminal's worried-looking girlfriend. Kissing noises in the back seat. Odd silences. Mom's giggle.

While away on trips with Vance, she often took me to Aunt Lu's apartment to spend the weekend. Upon dropping me back at home one Sunday, Lu walked through the front door and gasped. "Oh my god, the house was robbed!"

The sliding glass door in the dining room had been shattered, and our living areas looked as if a fraternity had thrown a keg party. Lu called the police, who dusted for fingerprints on the bar glasses left sitting about, some of which had lipstick on the rims. "Can you identify people from their lip prints?" I asked one of the officers.

"You watch too much television," he said.

A few weeks later, Mom told me it was Dan who had broken in. He'd come to the house with a woman and a few male buddies, smashed through the glass door, and loaded up what he wanted into a U-Haul. He and his helpers then had quite a party. He even allowed two of my grandmother's oil paintings to be taken from my room: one of a guardian angel she'd said visited her when she was a child, and another painting she'd done of a little girl whispering in a dog's ear.

I no longer felt physically safe in the house and began to have a recurring dream that lions, tigers, and alligators lived in our backyard. They waited, stock-still and staring, poised for attack. As I ran to the sliding glass door, the one Dan had smashed, the animals charged. I could never get the lock to turn in time to save myself, and the dream ended in terror when the animals were upon me, ready to kill.

Before yet another trip together, one for which Vance, a licensed pilot, intended to fly them himself, he and Mom arrived at the hangar and discovered the tires on his plane had been slashed. But Mom had a trick or two up her own sleeve. I rode with her to Dan's music store one evening after ballet. She parked by the curb on the side street near the warehouse area. "Stay here," she said. "I'm going to break in."

It was a windy night, and the huge trees on the street swayed ominously, making the dim streetlights seem to flicker on and off through the leaves. It was also a particularly dark night, and Mom's tiny figure was a vague shadow at the door. While she worked to jimmy the lock, a police car approached, then slowed. Mom switched to a more casual body language, as if she had a key in her hand, not a metal fingernail file. The police officer watched her momentarily, then drove on. She gained access to the building, went into Dan's office, and removed documents she thought might be of help to her in the divorce. I never learned if Dan suspected or accused her.

Changes came at a dizzying speed. I didn't get to say goodbye to Angela before she returned to Mexico, and I never saw her again. Her room, which had been such a haven, felt empty and gloomy. My goldfish died, followed soon by the death of my parakeet. Mom took our cats and their kittens to the pound one day while we were at school. She cleaned out our bedrooms and threw away what she didn't want us to keep. Greyson went to live with Dad and Patsy; I never knew why. I lay in bed at night and prayed to God to please, please make Dan return so we could all pick up where we'd left off. He was the only father I'd ever known, and he told me he loved me every night when he tucked me in and kissed me. Surely it meant he did.

Up to that point, all events in the house were framed in turquoise—how could they not be—but a darkness moved in, imprinting that time upon me in black and white. Our home seemed to lose its energy and brightness, as if a storm loomed outside. Mom put the house on the market, and it sold within weeks.

As I rode with her throughout Houston for my ballet lessons and her endless errands, she gushed about Vance and how wonderful it was to be with him. "When he puts his arm out on the seat like this, I know what it *really* means. He wants me to hold his hand," she said, demonstrating. I wondered why he didn't simply reach for her hand instead of pretending his had by some freak accident ended up near hers. "I'm so glad I can talk to you," she said, squeezing my fingers.

I valued my new role as twelve-year-old confidante more than almost anything. I hadn't told Dan about the many visits to

Vance's office, or the lunch at the cafeteria, or the back-seat date at the drive-in theater, for to do so risked the forfeit of the special role I played for Mom. Nor had I told Mom about Dan's nightly wet kisses or his hands up my nightgown. I knew not to look to her for protection, for never once did I see her stand up to him. His actions where Greyson and I were concerned were never up for discussion. All decisions were final. Still, my allegiance lay squarely with Dan, who lavished so much attention on me. From where I stood, Mom had ruined everything by having an affair. For whatever my childhood had or had not been under Dan's rule, it was familiar and at least navigable. More than anything, I wanted to go back to the time before I betrayed him, for surely my silence about the affair made me as guilty as Mom.

A few weeks after he left, I asked Mom for permission to call him. When he answered the phone, I burst into tears. "Daddy? I miss you. Can I please see you?"

"My therapist said no. He said you remind me too much of your mother."

"Okay," I choked out, and hung up.

One day while riding my bicycle around the neighborhood, I turned my head toward the honking horn of a car passing me on the left. It was Dan, and something undefinable in the relaxed and smiling demeanor of the woman with him suggested she was his girlfriend. There had been no word from him since my phone call. I'd sent a letter a few weeks before but heard nothing back. I waved, steered my bike to the curb, and waited for him to pull over. He smiled big, waved, and kept driving. Stunned, I watched the back of his car disappear into traffic.

A few weeks later, he allowed me to visit him at his new apartment. It was unorganized and sparsely furnished. There was no organ or piano, and it seemed both of us were at a loss as to how to occupy our time together. His apartment was on a high floor in the building, so I entertained myself by making frequent trips out into the hallway, summoning the elevator, and riding up and down after pushing the button for every floor. No doubt the residents who stepped on were a bit ticked off and inconvenienced, but no one accused me of anything. I stepped off onto the next floor as if nothing were amiss, waited for the doors to close, summoned the elevator again, then started the game anew.

Dan informed me of his divorce strategy during the visit. He said he'd consulted Richard "Racehorse" Haynes—a legendary defense attorney—about representing him. Haynes didn't, as a rule, handle divorces; he'd made a name for himself with high-profile murder cases. But Dan said he wanted an attorney willing to go for blood. What blood he thought he could get from Mom was beyond my comprehension, but his need for revenge was palpable; he had to somehow make her pay dearly.

Never during the time he was my stepfather, nor thereafter, did I hear him confess a mistake, a personal shortcoming, or the opinion that he'd ever behaved improperly in his life. Mom said she and Dan saw a therapist a few times before the discovery of her affair, and each had a private session at least once. "The therapist told me Dan thinks his shit doesn't stink," Mom told me.

He invited me out to lunch every few months after the divorce and never failed to deliver emotional bombshells I couldn't process. "Your mother didn't want custody of you and Greyson. I convinced her to keep you," he said. I wasn't sure I believed him. How could Mom not want us? What defects did we have that made her want to give us away? "I never liked Greyson," Dan said. "And I didn't care if he liked me. The way I saw it, the marriage was always just you, me, and your mother."

I realized I'd sensed it all along. Dan flat-out ignored Debbie and Jimmy. He'd beaten Greyson far more often than he'd beaten me. I'd had a starring role in the home: the singing, dancing little shining star—touched, kissed, secretly photographed—Dan's prized and subdued possession.

"Do you think I should marry Lu?" he asked while driving me home after a lunch together.

"Nah," I said. "She's too whiny."

"Yeah, maybe you're right," he said. "But she sure is a screamer in bed."

Mr. Jenkins—my ballet teacher—had expressive blue eyes that missed nothing. Slender and fit, with a physique that never changed, he seemed ageless. He maintained a calm and well-modulated tone, until his playful side appeared, during which his jokes became louder, his smile grew bigger, and his voice turned both throaty and gushy through his laughter.

He'd call out my name, plus my last name, then tack on Mom's accumulated marital names at the end. No one else could tease me in such a way and make me smile. His touch as he adjusted an arm, a hand, the tilt of my head, calmed me. I knew no other man like him.

The advanced ballet class finished around seven at night. One evening after all the other students had left, Mr. Jenkins had an engagement to attend. Instead of being able to shower, change clothes, and possibly make it there on time, he felt compelled to sit with me until Mom arrived. Not comfortable leaving me outside in the dark, he often waited with me before locking up the studio. As we sat together that night, he frequently checked his watch, then looked at me in a way I could hardly bear. "I'm really going to have to go soon," he said.

I nodded and looked around the paneled room at all the ballerina photos covering the walls. "Who's that?" I asked.

"Fonteyn."

"Um, who's that?" I said, pointing.

"Makarova."

If I saw the slightest bit of exasperation when I asked, I gave it a rest for a while.

"I have to leave soon," he said, looking at his watch.

"Who's this one?" I pointed. I couldn't move him away from flat, perfunctory answers and had no other ideas for how to deflect his anger. We were stuck in that small room together, and he grew more perturbed by the minute. "Um . . . that one?" I said, pointing to a photo.

He shifted in his chair and looked at his watch again. By now, he'd been waiting with me for over thirty minutes. His expression was stony. "I'm going to be late."

"Why don't I wait on the front patio?"

He looked through the glass door and out into the parking lot, looked back at me, and seemed to consider the possibility.

"I'll wait behind the wall. I promise I'll stay right there," I said.

"All right," he said, sighing. "But please be careful. I really do have to go."

"Okay, I'll stay right there," I said. I took my dance bag and stepped outside.

"*Please* ask your mother to be on time from now on!" he said, locking the door behind me.

I stood behind the decorative concrete grating on the front walkway and hid there until Mom arrived, about ten minutes later. I got in the car quickly, swung the door shut, and looked over at her. The cab light was on, illuminating her face. "Mr. Jenkins said you need to be on time from now on."

She rolled her eyes.

Dan had always decided which arts to pursue and the lessons I'd undertake, and it didn't occur to me to pare back on the number of activities after he left. I participated in every school assembly, play, concert, talent show, and musical, along with twice-weekly ballet lessons and the church choir. Since the school music program provided built-in friends, I never had to worry about who I associated with or endure lunchroom trauma regarding where I sat. Music provided three years' protection from most public-school suffering.

My music teacher devoted a tremendous amount of time to me. She and her husband, who was one of the nicest men to ever set foot on earth, were childless, and they showered me with attention. They invited me to their home for dinner or took me out to eat; she bought birthday presents for me and even let me sleep overnight at their home a few times. But once again, I was under the rule of someone who demanded perfection. "I'm not giving you the lead in the musical if you have braces on your teeth," my teacher warned. "There's no way I'm putting you up there with a mouth full of metal." Mom canceled my first orthodontist appointment, which had required a six-month wait.

My teacher grabbed the lower layer of my new shag haircut and shook it back and forth. "What's all this mess down here?" she asked, frowning. She subjected me to long lectures about how I was required to look and behave. "More is expected from you than other students," she'd explain. "You must set an example. You just smile if other students are mean."

Her frustration peaked when I suffered from grass allergies one spring and could barely sing. I developed stabbing stomach pains and psychosomatic illnesses, going so far as to lose my voice for days until I walked onstage and started to perform.

On the morning she saw Mike, a fellow music student, put his arm around me in the hall, she abruptly pulled me aside. "How *dare* you let a boy disrespect you like that!"

I feigned indifference toward him that morning as we sat at the piano together in choir, and he withdrew his attention permanently.

"Remember," she said, "someone is always watching."

"Always?" I asked, confused as to how that could be.

"Always."

When my English teacher told me I'd fallen behind on a project, I slumped in my desk and let out a long sigh. She sent a note home to Mom, labeling me a defeatist. New to teaching and new to our school, she knew little about me. I was anything but a defeatist but still couldn't discern exactly *what* I was. The turmoil in my head kept spinning, and I continued to push through the days.

One day I stayed after school, probably for a rehearsal. It had been a long and tedious day, the kind that needed to end, and I was already particularly agitated when Mom arrived to pick me up. Instead of heading home, she turned in the opposite direction, toward the freeway. "Where are you going?" I asked.

"I have to return this curtain tassel," she said, picking it up and waving it. The fringed gold tassel had remained in her car for who knew how many weeks, so long that it presented itself as a permanent resident of the front seat. Because of the dire need to return the tassel to its rightful place that very day, we were on our way downtown at the start of Houston's afternoon traffic. We were two miles from home.

"Let me out. I'll walk," I said.

"Just go with me."

"Let me out. I'll just meet you at home," I said. I looked ahead, then looked at her, waiting for her to pull over, but she kept driving. "I don't want to go with you, I want to go home. Let me out of the car!" I opened the car door and attempted to jump out.

Mom was wide-eyed with disbelief. "Cissie!" she yelled, hitting the brake.

The sight of the rapidly moving pavement under my extended foot caused me to reconsider. I leaned back into the car and swung the door closed. "Why can't you just take me home?" I said, clutching the door handle and considering how I might escape.

"Just go with me," she said.

"I don't want to go with you!"

But she refused to drop me off at the house. It was already after four in the afternoon, and we were on our way downtown to return a tassel. I settled into my fuming resentment and stared out the window, silent, for the entire two hours.

"What seems to be the problem?" Dr. Buie asked.

Mom sat on the front edge of the child psychiatrist's couch, gently holding her purse on her lap. With her body angled, ankles crossed, and spine so erect, she looked posed for a *Life* magazine photo shoot. When she began to speak, I noticed she'd left her southern drawl somewhere out in the waiting room.

"Cissie has become quite belligerent," she said, with precise enunciation.

Mom rarely used big words, and certainly not to describe my behavior. When she wanted me to lose some sass, she often called me Miss Priss. "You can just get down off your high horse, young lady," she might add. She talked for a few minutes about the hostility I frequently lobbed at her. "It's so unlike Cissie, this new behavior. Not like her at all."

She made no mention of the divorce or her new marriage. Dr. Buie was good friends with Vance and no doubt already had the backstory. Mom left the room so the doctor and I could talk privately. He put paper and crayons on the coffee table in front of me. "Draw a picture of anything you want. Anything at all," he said.

I was twelve years old and viewed crayons as a bit beneath me, but I let it slide. I drew Vance's face, although my drawing skills were so poor, no one could have known without my having written VANCE at the bottom of the page. Dr. Buie took the drawing, inserted it in a manila folder, and placed it off to the side.

During the sessions that followed, he rarely ever moved. He sat with an ankle propped on the opposite knee, his elbows on the arms of his chair, and his fingers interlocked and resting against his chest. He didn't say a word. I sat on the couch across from his chair, swinging my legs back and forth, with nothing to do but study every feature of the small windowless room. His glasses further magnified his large dark eyes and caused his expression to always register surprise, even when at rest. When I looked at him, he quickly looked away, and the darting about of his eyes made him appear to be on temporary high alert. After a few weeks of mind-numbingly boring appointments, I could take no more. "Is this all we're gonna do?" I asked.

"It's your time. We'll do what you want," he said.

I'd spent hours staring at a stack of board games on the small bookcase behind him. "Let's play Battleship," I said.

For fifty minutes every week, I sat on the floor on my side of the coffee table and tried to sink his ships. He was a formidable opponent. After several sessions of this, I asked that the picture I'd drawn of Vance be returned to me. I tore it up and handed it back. I had never said a word in the sessions about my home situation or what I felt, but at that moment, Dr. Buie finally started talking. "The problems you're dealing with are too adult for you. You're not allowed to be a child. Go home and play. Climb a tree."

When Mom picked me up after the appointment, I slid into the front seat of her Cadillac and told her what he'd said. She rolled her eyes. I had no further appointments with Dr. Buie but never asked why.

Greyson's departures and arrivals weren't always fully explained. He left Dad and Patsy's house and moved with us to our newly

constructed townhome about a mile from the turquoise wonderland, which had been sold during the divorce. Vance, Mom,
Greyson, and I lived in a sea of avocado-green and mandarin-or-
ange decor, only a notch or two down from turquoise and purple
on the sensory-assault scale.

Vance had to have wondered what the hell kind of bomb he
set off in his life. His ex-wife and their four children were left
reeling. His Catholicism engendered gnawing guilt; he believed
there could be no forgiveness for his sin of divorce. Greyson preferred to deal with his hostility by remaining closed up in his
room playing rock music at deafening volume. I viewed Mom and
Vance as the sole cause for my unhappiness and the oppressive
tension in our home, and assigned full blame to them for the dis-
appearance of a stepfather who I believed loved me. I interpreted
Vance's abrupt transition from virtual stranger to stepfather as an
enemy invasion. I barely knew him.

Facing so many challenges from so many fronts gave Vance
and Mom no time to enjoy life as newlyweds or develop a firm
foundation. When the tension in our home became unbearable,
the four of us saw various family therapists who got us nowhere.
It was time to recruit the big guns, and Vance knew of a psychologist with an impressive following. I had, coincidentally, seen
him on local television once before, providing group marriage
counseling. He seemed like a cool guy and was a bit of a celebrity
in the area.

The monthly bill for our family of four must have been staggering. Mom and Vance attended group marriage counseling
with other couples. Greyson and I attended group counseling
with other teens. We also had individual sessions from time to
time.

Our family's therapy was strongly influenced by the zeitgeist
of the seventies, an era of "being real" and "sharing." Our therapist believed in physical touch during sessions, and he expected

the members of our teen group to sit close to one another on the huge circular couch and hold hands. I did not like boys touching me and resented this sanctioned free access to my body. Such intimate contact hinted at sexual, and I felt nowhere near ready to explore my fear of it. During my private sessions with the doctor, he sat close to me on a small love seat in his office, put his arm around me, and snuggled while the two of us talked. I confided my fear of boys. I was afraid that if I spent any time alone with them, they might try to kiss me.

"You don't think it would be exciting to have a guy run his tongue across your lips?" he asked, slowly tracing the edges of my mouth with his index finger.

"Um. No."

Normally staid and reserved, Vance had found a new milieu. When not practicing medicine, he practiced giving "warm fuzzies"—which were compliments, reassuring touches, or hugs—and saying, "Right on, man" when he felt others "just let it all hang out."

Our therapist believed little was out-of-bounds in word or deed as long as it was "honest." Vance may as well have flicked acid on my skin every time he victimized me with his honesty. "Your perfume makes me horny," he told me.

As I lay stretched out on the couch one afternoon, staring out the sliding glass door at the trees behind the townhouse, Vance sat down, then moved close enough to press his thigh against my foot. "Your foot just feels so good!" he said, squirming like an excited puppy. When I pulled my foot away, he laughed and shook his head, for rejecting someone's touch meant you were "uptight" per our therapist. I got up from the couch and left the room.

There was insufficient physical or emotional space for me. Vance could do little that did not annoy me. The hip-hugger blue-and-white-striped bell-bottom jeans he wore with black dress shoes and a wide white belt embarrassed me. Or the way he sat with his legs crossed like a woman, his hands forming a fussy little cup over his crotch. Even the way he said my name—sandpaper on my already raw nerves. When I came downstairs for breakfast every morning, morose and sleep-deprived as always, he affected an exaggeratedly cheerful expression. "Well, good morning, Thithy!" he'd call out. He and Mom laughed when my face registered disgust.

I wanted to fall to my knees and beg, literally beg, for space, for air, for privacy, to get out of my goddamned head, to stop with the touchy-feely crap, to give me time to process the loss of Dan, Angela, and our turquoise home. There was an ever-looming sense that I couldn't cope much longer. I wanted to scream that I was only thirteen years old, for god's sake. *Leave me be for a while. Give me time to somehow emerge from this convoluted mass of emotional hell. Back away from me. I am desperate for you to back away from me. It's all too much. YOU are too much.* But I couldn't access words, I could only access anger.

Because there were few boundaries at home, my armor went up as soon as I walked in the door. I cut off Mom's access to my inner emotional world; she found herself entirely banned. She continued to surprise-clean Greyson's and my rooms while we were at school, and all items thought unnecessary were thrown away. My personal possessions in the house consisted of clothes, a clock radio, some jewelry, and a Bible.

As I sat on a doctor's exam table, I considered asking him private questions about the weird changes in my body. But before I got the chance, Mom came in from the waiting room, threw open the door without even a knock, breezed in, and took a seat. "Cissie is quite concerned about not starting her menstrual period yet," she said.

As a teenage girl, few things were more horrifying—and few things I strove harder to avoid—than embarrassment. It often took days for the mental tape of an incident to stop playing in my head, and my brain habitually zeroed in on the slightest twinge of self-consciousness and morphed it into full mortification. This was one of those times. She was lucky I was still fully dressed, for to allow her to ever see me without clothes was unthinkable. I shared *nothing* with her, not my sadness, growing loneliness, successes or failures at school, therapy sessions, or even the rare times in which I might have experienced joy. And so, I never allowed her a view of my naked body, as it might imply I felt an iota of trust or rapport. Nudity had at some point come to represent vulnerability, and I revealed my naked body to no one. Not friends, not classmates in gym class, not girls and women in the ballet studio dressing room.

Mom and the doctor proceeded to talk about me as if I weren't there. I vowed not to speak to her for days, but in the car on the way home, my anger boiled over. "Why did you do that?" I said.

"Do what?" she said, looking confused.

"Barge in like that! I had questions I wanted to ask him."

"What questions?" she asked.

"Just questions, okay?"

"But what kind of questions did you want to ask him?"

"Just things."

"But you can ask me questions," she said, looking hurt.

"Forget it. No way!"

I got my first period a few months later but didn't tell her. When she found out by accident and confronted me, I burst into tears, resenting that anything personal about my life had been shared with her without my consent. She told Vance I'd started, and he thought it was a good idea to mention it to me. "Why did you tell him?" I asked Mom angrily.

"Well, because he's a doctor," she said.

"Why are you telling him about my cramps?" I asked her a few months later.

"Because he's a doctor!"

I saw no reason for him to have access to such personal information about my body. My resentment continued to grow as his therapy-driven attempts at "connecting with me" increased.

When Dan appeared one day after scheduling lunch with me, I swung the door open and threw my arms around him. "Daddy!" I cried out.

Mom said that after I left, Vance lay down on the bed and cried. "She never treats me that way," he said. And the more I pulled away from him, the harder he tried to pull me back.

Chapter Six

On the first day of high school, I stepped out of the cafeteria lunch line with my tray, looked out onto a sea of hundreds of faces, and realized with horror that I had no clique. I no longer had a predetermined place to sit. Worse, my two best girlfriends attended school in a different district. I went to a table at the far corner of the room and saw Lisa and Amy, two girls I barely knew from junior high. "Is it okay if I sit here?" I asked. They looked at each other and shrugged. My presence seemed to make their conversation stilted, and they made no effort to talk to me. From then on, I bought hard-boiled eggs and V-8 juice at the snack bar and ate alone every day in an outdoor courtyard. I ran on the girls' track team and continued ballet lessons but grew more and more solitary.

Dr. Buie, my ex–Battleship-playing child psychologist, told Vance about a young woman he knew who had attended Interlochen Arts Academy, a fine arts boarding school in Michigan. Mom and I filled out an application and sent an audition tape. I was accepted as a voice major for my sophomore year. The school afforded intense study of the arts, with the added benefit of being over a thousand miles from home.

Without me in the house, Mom and Vance could focus on their relationship, which had become increasingly strained. "He wants to put me on a budget of one hundred dollars a month," she said. "That's supposed to cover my clothes, hair and nail appointments, makeup, everything."

"Are you gonna do it?" I asked.

She smirked.

If she played the piano for dinner guests, he appeared bored and restless. He also resented the baby talk and endless affection she showed our Pomeranian. "He told me I have an abnormal attraction to Lulu," Mom said.

When she ran late one evening at the salon, she called and told me to relay a message to him as soon as he walked in the door. "Make sure you tell him I'm on my way," she said.

Yeah, whatever.

A short while later he came home, but I didn't care to rush downstairs. I heard his quick steps across the kitchen tile, the slam of the door, and his car driving away. A few minutes later, Mom walked into the house with a confused look on her face. Vance was always home by that time in the evening.

"Sorry, Mom. I heard him come in but didn't get downstairs fast enough."

"That's okay," she said, sighing.

Loud voices coming from the master bedroom downstairs woke me one night. I couldn't hear what they were saying, only that there was a great deal of back-and-forth shouting. Their voices abruptly stopped. Mom came into my bedroom and wordlessly crawled under the covers. The next morning, I was surprised to see them dressed and ready to play tennis. Mom wore a sleeveless outfit that in no way covered the developing bruise on her bicep. After breakfast, I walked with them to the end of the subdivision to watch them play tennis. They were in surprisingly good spirits, smiling often and showing affection toward one another. It struck me that the public display of her bruise, which grew alarmingly black as the days passed, was Mom's official warning to him.

Before I left for school, Vance had one more plan up his sleeve for some do-it-yourself family therapy. He flew the four of us in his plane to Ely, Minnesota, where he'd contracted with one of the outfitting companies that specialized in canoeing and camping vacations. Vance felt we needed more togetherness. Team spirit. Pulling together. Working toward a common goal.

We arrived in Ely at the height of mosquito season. As we waited for the company to load our personal belongings, tents, food, and gear for transport to our site, a forest ranger gave us pointers about camping in the area. A swirl of gray surrounded his face and neck, and any exposed skin was dotted with bites. "How do you stand the mosquitoes?" I asked, noting that several more had landed on him in the short time it took me to ask.

"You get used to it," he said, not even bothering to swat.

A man from the outfitting company loaded us into a boat that carried our canoes on an overhead rack, then deposited us at a site chosen for us beforehand. Mom and Vance proved surprisingly adept at pitching their tent, while Greyson and I fumbled around with ours, gave up, then stood around dully reviewing our situation. What to do, what to do. There was nothing to do, that's what. The water was so deep it looked like black ink, and its temperature was far too cold for swimming. Greyson and I went out in a canoe the next day and were caught in an unexpected storm so forceful that we didn't have time to get back to the campsite before it hit. The exertion of paddling against the wind brought us to the point of exhaustion, but the storm calmed right when we gave up.

The mosquitoes became a nightmare. We used OFF! spray liberally, even on our faces, and in such high humidity, we were rendered sticky, sweaty, and oily. Our food was freeze-dried. Mealtimes were at least something to look forward to, as boiling water became the high point of my day. I tried to fish but only caught a few five-inch-long something-or-others, which I threw back in the lake. Not one of us ever even hiked around, we were so in shock about being forced into such close proximity twenty-four hours a day. There were no other campers near us, and we never saw anyone pass by on the lake. We were on our own, and heaven forbid we'd had a life-threatening emergency. We didn't sit around the fire, and we didn't play games. We barely spoke to each other. To top it off, my brother and I had to share a tent. On the third night, an argument broke out between us, and we started punching and kicking one another through our sleeping bags.

The next day, all agreed it was a one-hundred-percent, through and through, family therapy/vacation/fun fail. For hours, the four of us took turns keeping close watch from the shore. It was the most cooperation we'd ever shown one another. When we saw a guide from the outfitting company passing by in a boat, we yelled, we jumped up and down, we waved clothing. You'd have thought our plane had gone down months before, requiring us to nibble on corpses to survive. When he spotted us and turned toward our campsite, we whooped with joy. It took us only minutes to be packed and ready to go.

"You didn't hang your food in a tree? We warn everyone to hang their food," the guide said.

"Why?" I asked.

"Bears. Lots of bears."

Ah, well, bears were the least of our worries.

A few weeks later, at the age of fifteen, I left for Interlochen. I planned to be a voice major, but when I auditioned in the group tryouts for dance, the teacher convinced me to change my major to ballet.

I must have been a sight. Farrah Fawcett hair, inch-long hot-pink fingernails, skin-tight bell-bottom jeans, four-inch platform shoes, and green eyeshadow to top off the look. I all but bathed in Charlie perfume. My appearance might have been acceptable in Texas, but not in Michigan. On one of my first report cards, which required students to comment about their semesters, I wrote, "I don't really feel like I fit in here."

But in the important ways, I did. My dance teacher accepted my forceful style of movement and worked with it. I made a lot of friends, most of whom were gay. The semester passed without incident, but more and more something felt off, like a heavy darkness descending. I'd grown restless. Mentally hyper. Agitated about nothing I could pinpoint. It was as if I couldn't bear to be in my own skin any longer, as if my own life felt claustrophobic, pressing in on me, making me want to escape not only the school but myself. Depression replaced agitation, only to cycle back again. Toward the end of the semester, about an hour before our final dance performance of the year, a realization came upon me. *I can't stay here.*

Perhaps I did what many teens do and attributed *place* as the cause of unhappiness, not forces within. Wherever I went, well, there I was. The school year ended, and I returned to Houston. I auditioned at High School for Performing and Visual Arts and was accepted as a dance major for the fall semester of my junior year.

One day during the summer, Mom and I strolled through the Galleria, a huge first-of-its-kind mall off Westheimer Road. Shopping was her favorite pastime, and she could press on from the time the stores opened in the morning until late in the afternoon, when she needed to head home to make dinner. It seemed during school breaks and summers, she and I were all each other had. She didn't pal around with girlfriends for lunch or shopping, and I had no one else with whom I could have done so. My friends were spread across other states, not to be seen again until semesters resumed. I still had no driver's license and relied on Mom far more than I wanted to.

We most often browsed through shoe stores or she tried on dress after dress she never bought. I trudged along desultorily, plodding through the overwhelming scents of cosmetic departments and carpet fumes, the air-conditioning so icy it seemed to freeze my sweat, followed by repeated entry into our one-hundred-and-forty-five-degree Houston-baked car to go to other shopping centers.

"Pick out some shoes you like and try them on," Mom said. "I'll be right back." She walked out of the store, and I asked a saleslady to bring my size in a cute pair I found. They fit, so there was nothing further to do but sit and wait. After fifteen minutes or so, I went to the doorway, looked both ways down the concourses for a while, then went back and sat down.

"Is there anything else I can get for you?" the saleslady asked.

"No. Thanks. Just waiting for my mom."

Tired of watching people come and go past the glass storefront, I stepped out of the store again. There were so many places she could have gone; the mall was multilevel and so large it even housed an ice-skating rink. To wander away in search of her was unthinkable. Wherever she left me, it was understood that was where I had to be when she returned. I went back to my chair.

There were mothers and daughters—at least I assumed they were—passing by with a relaxed ease of being in each other's company. A young girl looked up at the woman next to her and smiled at something she'd said. People of all ages wandered by in twos or small groups, apparently happy to spend hours at the mall. Enjoying being at a mall was an inconceivable concept to me, but a sense of belonging might have made it worthwhile. However, it was achingly obvious that any friendship vacancies left open by my going away to school in another state had been quickly filled. I'd tried to reconnect with a neighbor across the street with whom I'd been close. "I'm sorry I didn't keep in touch better," I said.

"That's okay. I have a new best friend now," she said, turning and walking away.

By now, nearly an hour had passed in the shoe store with no sign of Mom. The saleslady no longer sent inquiring looks my way but went about her job, working around my presence. Once again, I went to the doorway to keep watch. I thought I saw her rather far away, coming out of Neiman Marcus. As the woman neared, she looked less and less like Mom, but there was no mistaking her tiny body, her DD bust, and the perky way she walked in high heels. She saw me watching her and broke out into a big smile.

She'd bought a wig—a short, high-at-the-crown, frosted-blonde, highlight-streaked pageboy wig with bangs. I couldn't stop staring at her, speechless, as she paid for the shoes I no longer liked but resented. The smile never left her face as we made our way to the parking lot. She looked as cute as a bug in that wig. I had never seen her look more beautiful. "I hate it," I said when we got in the car. She frowned for a second, but her smile returned. She put on her dark, oversized sunglasses before starting the engine. At that moment, there wasn't a movie star in the world who could have held a candle to her. "It looks so stupid," I said. As she started the drive home, there was still a hint of a smile on her lips. "God, you look terrible," I said.

The remaining touch of a smile faded further, then disappeared altogether. If she ever wore the wig again, I never saw it.

Chapter Seven

I rode with her to an area clear on the other side of town, out by the Houston ship channel, for one of her errands. She had to turn the car around after getting lost, and we came within several feet of a group of sailors. "Smile and wave at 'em, honey," she said. "They haven't seen a pretty girl all day!"

They smiled and waved back enthusiastically. At the age of fifteen, I'd transitioned into a more mature stage of development, one in which adult men found me attractive. It didn't hurt that the clothes Mom bought or passed down to me had me dressed to the nines. It was one thing to attract high school boys, but grown men? I was intrigued. A pack of sailors? What a heady feeling. I wanted males to like me, and Mom taught me how to earn their attention. She'd delivered these lessons to me over the many years we'd ridden in the car together throughout Houston.

A man can tell a lot about a woman by looking at her hands.

A man doesn't like it when a woman dresses too sexy.

A man likes a woman to be a bit of a challenge. Play a little hard to get.

Don't compliment a man too soon. Make him work for it.

Never be dependent on a man for money.

It's just as easy to fall in love with a rich man as a poor man.

That same summer, Mom and Vance invited a couple over for dinner. Vance had performed surgery on the man, which didn't explain why they were having dinner with us, as he didn't make a habit of socializing with patients. But his wife taught modeling classes, and Mom asked her if I could enroll. The wife agreed and referred us to a photographer, a man named Randy, to take a few shots of me for a portfolio.

I guessed his age to be late twenties. He wore an orange long-sleeved shirt with a large collar. Orange polyester bell-bottom pants. Platform shoes. With his shaggy haircut and big brown puppy-dog eyes, he could not have looked more like Sonny Bono. He spent about ten minutes with me, calling out a few ideas for poses and clicking away. I followed his instructions, struck a pose, and held it. "So. What do you think about me taking you out sometime?" he asked, looking at me through the camera lens.

"Let me ask my mom." I went out to the waiting room and told her he'd asked me for a date.

"That'll be fine," she said.

I'm not sure under what pretense we ended up back at his photography studio one evening. The parking lot was empty, and the building was dark. When we entered the main photography area, he led me to a closet with a makeshift bed, a cassette tape player, and a small lamp on the floor. I didn't think to ask why he needed a bed at his workplace, but I lay down with him anyway. While we kissed, which he said I did quite badly, he repeatedly tried to force his hand between my legs. "Have you ever felt anything like this before?" he asked. Apparently, he mistakenly thought he had broken through my clenched thighs and might soon bring me to orgasm. "Like when riding your bicycle?" he added.

"No," I said, thinking riding my bicycle sounded like a lot more fun. I continued to push his hand away and refused to do more than kiss.

I didn't have the slightest bit of attraction to him but dated him a few more times. Whenever we were together, he begged me to have sex with him. He pleaded, urged, then demanded. I continued to say no. He gave me an ultimatum. "If you keep refusing, I'll have to take matters into my own hands." I told him to enjoy his hand and never heard from him again.

At the end of that summer, I started the fall of junior year at High School for Performing and Visual Arts in Houston. My athletic style of dance frustrated Gil—the ballet teacher—to no end. Knowing I had to endure an hour-and-a-half dance class with him daily made getting up in the morning sheer hell. He spent the entire semester demanding I pull back my strength—pull it back all the way to Cleveland. Loud, impatient, and condescending, he often stopped class to belittle me. "No! You're going to do it *my* way!" he'd yell. It never occurred to me to speak to him about it, nor did I ever discuss the problem with Mom or Vance. They, in turn, never asked if the choice of school proved to be a good one.

The depression and agitation still hung over me like a shroud, and my sleep pattern turned erratic. I dragged through the days exhausted but was too wired by nighttime to fall asleep. I'd lost a surprising amount of hair. And I'd developed yet another issue: inexplicable weight gain. It wasn't as if I packed in calories. Vance preferred that Mom not buy steak or most other meats, plus his medical training told him fat in food was the enemy, so he was oddly content with a nightly dinner of steamed broccoli, cauliflower, or an artichoke. Not as a side dish, but as the main course. Mom served our single steamed vegetable with a loaf of French bread and called it a meal. There was no cafeteria at the high school, so many of us swarmed "the roach coach" truck that showed up every day around noon. Once again, I ate hard-boiled eggs for lunch. And still, I gained weight.

Dance majors were required from time to time to stand before the teachers for weight evaluation. They announced the verdict in the presence of the other dance students. I stood front and center as the head of the dance department sat in a chair and looked me up and down. "About eight pounds overweight," she said.

Exhausted, depressed, overweight, and studying dance under a man who seemed angered by my very presence in his class. Maybe Gil dedicated so much time to me because he saw something of value. Maybe he believed he could shape me into the kind of dancer he thought I could be. But his daily humiliations drove me even further inside myself, and it was all I could do to attend his class. Whenever someone taught in his place, I relaxed as if granted a temporary stay of execution. The semester had been such hell, I'd decided on the lesser of two evils, not knowing of any other choice. Mom and Vance agreed to send me back to Interlochen.

Toward the end of the one and only semester I attended HSPVA, Gil and I stood together in the school auditorium and watched a rehearsal for an upcoming performance. I don't recall how he found out that I'd chosen to leave. "I'm sorry to see you go," he said. "I really wanted to work with you."

I came home from school and found Mom puttering around in the kitchen. "Vance moved out," she said, not sounding at all upset.

"What? Why?"

"I asked him to meet me at the cafeteria, and I told him I wanted a divorce."

"What did he say?" I asked.

"He seemed relieved."

Yeah. You and me both.

Later that week, she asked me to stop by a certain department store near school and buy five pieces of luggage, a set she'd seen featured on sale in the newspaper. I charged it on her account, along with a dress and pair of shoes for myself. When the bill arrived a few weeks later, she about delivered a kitten on the kitchen floor. How dare I charge so much on the card! Her anger confused me; wasn't the cost of her luggage included? She called the store and pleaded for more time. "It'll take me a while, but I'll pay it off," she told a woman on the phone. "My daughter charged some things."

She didn't yet know when financial support kicked in, and her fear was palpable. There wasn't even child support to rely on, as Dad never sent a penny. I could understand why a large credit card bill upset her but couldn't see how I was entirely responsible. She hung up the phone and turned to face me. "Lu arranged for me to attend a Pipeliners Association convention so I can meet some men, and I'll have to buy gowns for the events. I can't afford to send you back to Interlochen."

An explosion went off in my head. My reaction scared her enough to call Lu for help.

"Cissie isn't on board with our idea," Mom told her. She listened for a moment, then handed the phone to me. "She wants to talk to you."

I put the receiver to my ear. Lu explained the need for my cooperation and support. "Uh-huh," I said. Surely, I could see how important it was for Mom to look particularly beautiful, couldn't I? "Uh-huh," I said.

Her closing argument was strident. "We're working hard to find you a father!" she said.

I handed the phone back to Mom. "I'll talk to you more about the trip later," she told Lu, then hung up.

I ran upstairs and called my biological father. "Dad, will you please come get me?" I asked.

"I'll be right there," he said.

When he pulled up to the house, I came downstairs and passed Mom as I went to the door. "I'm going to Dad's," I said.

"Oh, no you're not!" she said. A tug-of-war ensued. I tried

to jerk my arm out of her grasp, but my platform shoes gave me no traction. Mom and I had never engaged in a physical battle before, which made our bout shocking in itself. She dragged me across the kitchen like a resistant dog on a leash, and the sheer embarrassment of doing a forced moonwalk on the tile floor outweighed any consideration for her feelings. She burst into tears and let go of my arm. "I don't know what I'm gonna do with you anymore!" she said. She ran into her bedroom and shut the door.

I got in the car with Dad and told him about the conversation. "Aunt Lu says she's working really hard to find me a new father."

I'd never seen him laugh so hard. "You tell her you already have a father."

It was a pivotal event for us. Dad and I hardly knew one another, but I'd needed him, and he came through.

Mom attended the convention and came home all aglow. The new luggage and evening gowns worked their magic, and apparently so had she. She needn't have worried; she could have worn a potato sack and stolen the show. Petite, slender, gray-eyed, and with frosted-blonde hair, she was a knockout. She often studied her reflection in mirrors or store windows we passed. Her face relaxed and her mouth turned up in a slight smile. "Lookin' good right now," her expression seemed to say.

As I sat on a barstool in the kitchen, she told me a little about her trip. "I was supposed to meet Marvin, but it turns out he already has a girlfriend. So I ended up with Roy." I came home a few days later and found her going through the drawers in my bedroom. "I need a good picture of myself to send to him. Do you have any of me?"

Without Mom announcing a formal decision, and with no discussion between the two of us, Interlochen was somehow back on the table. I didn't ask how or why. When Vance and Mom had decided to send me back, only several weeks remained before the spring semester started, so re-enrollment and the payment of tuition were urgent to reserve my place and dormitory room. Return to Michigan I did, and I didn't ask how she afforded it. But within several weeks of my return to school, my letters to her included pleas for money. "Mom, please. *Please* send a check. I'm running out of everything." Soon, I resorted to stealing tampons from the boxes my suitemates left in the bathroom. I sneaked shampoo from the bottles they left in the shower, using as little as possible so the theft might go unnoticed. If I could borrow a stamp or two from someone, I occasionally wrote to Dad and explained, "Sorry it took me so long to respond to your letter. I couldn't afford to mail anything."

After seeing this comment a few times, he included a twenty-dollar bill in his reply. "I thought you were kidding," he wrote. "But the more I thought about it, the more I realized you might mean it." I wrote back and thanked him profusely for the cash. "Don't mention the money when you write, just tell me you got the letter," he responded. Dad's paycheck didn't go far, and Patsy apparently read the letters I sent him.

Mom called before spring break. "I can't afford to fly you home. You might have to stay with your ballet teacher." I said nothing but inwardly refused to consider any such imposition on a teacher, much less my favorite. Sure enough, Mom made reservations to fly me back to Texas. This time, however, I had to spend the entire spring break with her and Roy, whom I'd not yet met.

He was an oil pipeline contractor and supposedly had a few million to his name. Picture John Wayne with a small mustache. He talked slowly, wore his pants low, and due to ongoing back pain, swaggered. Mom soon confided that Roy had developed an addiction to Percodan. He ingested ten pills a day, accompanied by a daily fifth of bourbon and a five-pack-a-day Doral cigarette habit. He blamed the failure of his first marriage on "*her* drinking problem."

During the visit, Mom motioned me into the kitchen one morning and fed me my lines. I went back into the living room, put my arms around Roy's neck, and whispered in his ear, "I can't wait till you're my father." He stiffened slightly and nodded. He had to have known it was scripted, as I'd remained all but mute for days. Roy had three sons and was at a loss as to how to deal with a teenage girl. I was quiet and wary, and we'd had little to talk about. I wasn't a good enough actress to successfully portray wanting yet another man I hardly knew to become my "father." Released from weeks of boredom and tension, I returned to Interlochen after spring break.

Lack of money remained an issue. Mom wrote a letter to Dr. Hood, the director at Interlochen, requesting financial assistance. She mailed it to me and told me to give it to him personally. I saw him most mornings in the cafeteria, so I brought the letter with me from the dorm and followed him up to the tray deposit window after he finished eating breakfast. "My Mom wanted me to give this to you," I said, handing him the envelope. He opened it, read for only a few moments, then stopped. He gave me a withering look. A look I understood. One I felt I deserved. I'd never needed or received a single dollar of financial help for Interlochen tuition. Vance was a doctor and still my stepfather for all anyone knew. My clothes and shoes were obviously expensive. I wore a diamond ring on my left hand. I hadn't read the letter Mom wrote, but Dr. Hood's expression of disgust spoke volumes: that Mom and I took him for some sort of fool. He didn't know I couldn't afford stamps. He didn't know I stole tampons and shampoo. He didn't know I wore pointe shoes until the toes shredded. He turned and threw the letter in the trash.

The reasons for his reaction could only be supposition on my part, for he never spoke to me again after that morning. Our friendly, chatty relationship turned cold, and from then on, he acted as if the mere sight of me nauseated him. He grudgingly acknowledged my presence to a campus visitor one afternoon. "She's only moderately talented," he told the guest.

Mom's marriage to Vance officially terminated in May. The school year ended in June, and I returned to Houston for the summer. Mom took off for what I thought was a short visit, but it appeared she'd only come to town to pick me up at the airport and get me settled before leaving to live with Roy. I didn't see her for weeks on end. I got a waitress job at a coffee shop but had no driver's license yet, so I took a cab to and from work. I arrived for the lunch shift and often worked until after midnight. Then I stopped off next door at Fool's Gold, a country-western bar owned by an Iranian family. They could not have been nicer, and even though they probably knew I was underage, they let me in without charge whenever I wanted. They also gave me free alcohol.

Every place I went that summer, I went by cab. More than once, I ended up with the driver with only one leg. "Will you marry me if I promise to take care of you the rest of your life?" he asked.

"Um. No."

"Because I have good disability payments. I really do."

"No. No, thanks."

Another cab driver said the locks on the back doors didn't work and told me to sit up front with him. At a traffic light, he slid his hand across the seat toward me and let it rest by my thigh. "You can just let me off right there. Right there at the yarn shop," I said, pointing. I went in and told an employee what had happened, and a woman who overheard—a stranger—gave me a ride home.

At the coffee shop, older men constantly struck up conversations while I served them. "Oh, let's talk some more later," I said to any man particularly handsome or funny. I scribbled my name and phone number on a napkin and handed it over.

A customer in his sixties called one night. "What are you wearing right now, Sondra?"

"I can't believe you'd ask me that!" I said and hung up.

An import/export trader took me to dinner. I felt excruciatingly self-conscious and tongue-tied all evening, and the more uncomfortable I became, the more uncomfortable he then became. He gave up trying to make conversation. We had a silent dinner, then he drove me home. He turned to me with a small, kind smile. "Maybe in a few years," he said.

A man who looked exactly like Clark Gable took me to dinner. We hit it off like gangbusters. He was kind, funny, and a complete gentleman. He'd recently bought a new Cadillac, which he let me drive down Interstate 10 at night, all the way to Katy, Texas, while we chatted and smoked cigarettes. I didn't even have a driver's license yet. He behaved himself and seemed to take a genuine interest in my life.

While I attracted men, I was, at the same time, petrified of them. I had no actual sexual experience, having done little more than kiss. Nor did I have much emotional intelligence. I continued to go out with complete strangers, men who were decades older, and never considered how my behavior could have gotten me raped or killed. After finishing my waitress shift one night and ending up at the bar once again, a singer who regularly performed there acted as if he'd taken a liking to me. "I'd like to treat you to lunch at Elan. I'll call you tomorrow," he said.

Wow! Elan was only *the* hottest new restaurant in Houston. I waited by the phone all day. Literally by the phone. After waiting for a few more hours on Sunday, I finally gave up. The next time I saw the singer at the bar, I questioned why he didn't call. "My voice was a little hoarse," he said, placing a few fingers against his throat.

His lie stung, but Mom taught me to never let a guy know he'd hurt me. "Yeah, your voice doesn't sound as good tonight," I said.

I found a seat at a table before his next set started and struck up a conversation with a wide-eyed young woman eating popcorn. "I can't believe it," she said excitedly. "He said he wants to sit with me at the next break!"

"Who?" I asked.

"Him!" she said, pointing up to the singer who didn't call me. He looked down from the stage, saw the two of us sitting together, and frowned.

The neighbor across the street eventually reported my numerous late-night comings and goings to Mom, still living full-time with Roy. For the rest of the summer, she hired someone to stay overnight with me in the townhouse. A youngish-looking man with shaggy sandy-colored hair showed up at my door one evening. I let him in, and we stood in the kitchen for a few moments, staring at one another. His glasses were so filthy, he may as well have rubbed Vaseline on them every morning. "Where's your luggage?" I asked.

"I don't have any."

"How can you not have any?"

He shrugged. "I just don't."

"Not even a toothbrush?"

"I didn't bring one," he said.

"You didn't bring a toothbrush?" I asked, incredulously. He shook his head. "You have to have a toothbrush. You have to!"

He left for a few minutes, went to the drug store, and came back with a toothbrush. If he'd stuck around much longer,

I might have lectured him on the importance of flossing, as I was particularly fussy about such things. But a tan, sexy young woman with a tricked-out Camaro inexplicably replaced him. Each person Mom hired showed up, chatted a bit, and left me alone. Never once did they try to tell me what to do. There wasn't much of the summer left, so I worked more shifts at the coffee shop as the weeks passed. Mom called in August to wish me a happy sixteenth birthday. "So, you can go pick out that stereo you've been wantin'," she said.

"Oh, thanks," I said.

"I also wanted to tell you, Roy and I got married last weekend."

"I knew you would," I said, trying to sound pleased.

"So you and I will be moving here," she said.

The summer concluded with her marriage, our home being put on the market, our dog being given to my grandmother, and, yet again, Mom going through my room and discarding anything she believed unnecessary to pack and move. Greyson continued to live with Dad and Patsy until his graduation from high school. Roy agreed to pay my tuition for Interlochen. Back to Michigan I went for senior year.

Chapter Eight

I loved my jeans to fit tight but could barely zip them. I'd developed curves but thought they were unavoidable given my age and hormones. "Hold in your stomach!" my ballet teacher called out to me one morning in class. I tried.

Ads for Appedrine, an over-the-counter appetite suppressant, appeared regularly in magazines, and I bought a package the next time I took the weekly bus to Traverse City. Along with twice-daily doses of the pills, I limited food intake to four hundred calories a day. At times my hands shook so badly, I struggled to get a forkful of food to my mouth. I developed dry heaves. And I was hot, always inexplicably hot. I cracked a window open in a corner of the ballet studio, welcoming icy-cold air to flow over me as I worked the barre. Every building and room I entered felt stiflingly overheated. I tugged at my clothes, at times wanting to tear them from my body. No amount of sleep left me rested, although I might sleep fourteen hours at a stretch on the weekends. Barely able to get out of bed in the mornings, I dragged through life as if slogging through mud. I dreaded my days and resented the endless demands on my depleted energy.

When I returned "home" for school breaks, apparently no one noticed any change in me. Roy wanted Mom to be far stricter with me, so she put new rules in place, rules that felt as if they were just for show. "You're not leaving this house until you make your bed," Mom said.

It hardly mattered. I had no driver's license and knew no one there. I hid out in the downstairs bathroom, soaking in the tub for hours and sneaking cigarettes. I interacted with Roy—father du jour—only when necessary. He did not like me, and I made no effort to change his mind. "You can catch more flies with honey than you can with vinegar," he told me.

"I don't know why you don't try harder. You could have him eating out of the palm of your hand," Mom said.

Whatever.

Back at school the next semester, I injured my right ankle, permanently destroying the foot's ability to extend and properly arch. I pulled my left hamstring so severely that other dancers heard it pop. I didn't request to see a doctor, nor did anyone suggest the need. I took the SAT, so tired it seemed physically impossible to still be awake. The reading and writing sections were easy enough, but with embarrassingly insufficient competence in math, I'd opted to make an attractive design of choices on the answer sheet. Somewhere I'd learned "when in doubt, always choose C," so I filled in the C circle often with my pencil. I laid my head on the table in between sections, hoping to remain awake enough to hear the proctor's instructions to continue.

A recurring dream haunted me. I step into an elevator and push a button for a floor. I ascend slowly, then the cab closes in, tighter and tighter, wrapping me in a metal cocoon. The most terrifying part is the anticipation, for I know with all certainty what will happen. I ascend, slowly rolling and cartwheeling. The air is cut off; I'm blanketed in sweltering humidity. My arms are pinned to my sides; I can do nothing to save myself. In another variation of the nightmare, I skyrocket to the top—immobilized, spinning, and suffocating.

My boyfriend, Billy, became my touchstone at Interlochen. My base, my constant. No matter what turmoil roiled within me, he remained a steady, mature-beyond-his-years presence. His parents liked me well enough until Billy and I started dating. Then, I believe, they viewed me as a distraction for their gifted and only child.

They had an annoying habit of showing up unexpectedly on campus. As far as I knew, even Billy didn't know when they might appear. Mr. J, as I called him, wore the Interlochen uniform—a light blue shirt and dark blue corduroy pants—when he visited, and I could spot his pear shape and purposeful walk clear across campus. He never simply wandered; he had a place to be—always in Billy's orbit whether on or off campus. He had protruding brilliant-blue eyes and an intense gaze. I recognized a familiar and intimidating trait in his demeanor: there was never a doubt that he'd get his way.

Fiercely intelligent, his comments could be both biting and hilarious. I walked with him one morning past a line of dormitories, where we passed several boys making a giant penis out of snow. They'd even made a divot at the top for anatomical accuracy. They looked over at us casually as we passed but continued their artistry. "Looks like you boys are struggling a bit with your manhood," Mr. J called out.

I adored Mrs. J, one of the nicest women I'd ever met. Always gracious and smiling, she tolerated me following her around like a puppy.

Senior year brought additional stress. Many students performed senior recitals, participated in concerto competitions, and auditioned at conservatories throughout the country. Our conversations covered student names attached to prestigious schools.

"Did you hear? He got into Oberlin!"

"She applied as a dance major. They said she doesn't have the body," someone whispered to me.

"Frank got into Harvard!" my roommate said.

"Wow. No shit?" I responded.

Over winter break I auditioned for the new musical theater department at Carnegie Mellon University. When I returned to IAA for the start of the spring semester, I arrived past midnight and the dorm was mostly dark. My roommate happened to be by the front desk, which was barely lit by a small lamp. I pulled a large, thick envelope from my mailbox and stepped toward the dim light. The return address read: Carnegie Mellon University Office of the Registrar. My roommate looked over my shoulder as I tore open the envelope, pulled out the cover letter, and began to read aloud. "We are happy to inform you . . ." My roommate and I shrieked.

An IAA drama major, who auditioned at Carnegie but had not been accepted, started a rumor that I'd slept with a professor as part of my audition. But I still had not slept with anyone, not even Billy. He never pushed me to have sex; he let me be in whatever state of mind I needed to be, which at times was a jumbled mess of pinballing emotions. Still a junior, he had a year remaining at IAA. We didn't consider breaking up. When I graduated, it felt as if I'd lost my lifeline.

After graduation ceremonies, I flew to Texas. CMU required a physical prior to attendance, and Mom arranged for me to see a local doctor. He placed his fingers on the front of my neck and pressed several times. "How long have you had this nodule on your thyroid gland?"

"This what?" I said.

"Right here," he said, gently pressing. "Hold on a minute. I'll be right back."

When he left the room, I slid off the exam table and went to the mirror over the sink. I felt around on my throat and found a lump that felt like a Ping-Pong ball. I hadn't noticed until then that the right side of my neck stuck out farther than the left.

The nodule, I came to learn, had been present for years, slowly but inexorably destroying my metabolism. The weight gain, exhaustion, erratic sleep, loss of short-term memory, dry heaves, hair-trigger agitation, claustrophobia, dry skin, hair loss, and the sensation of living in an oven had an actual physical cause. Tests run the next day revealed my thyroid gland barely functioned.

I stayed with Dad and Patsy in Houston to await the endocrinologist appointment, which was weeks away. My malfunctioning thyroid gland lacked the ability to help regulate my temperature, and a blast furnace burned within me. Even though the summer temperatures soared well into the nineties, Patsy did not allow the use of the home air conditioner during the day due to the cost. Her economizing soon required us to drink coffee so weak as to be transparent and frozen orange juice made with twice the water required. She instructed us to save and reuse aluminum foil, plus rinse and dry Baggies, some of which could survive reuse for well over a year, she believed. Starting the washer or dryer with less than a full load bordered on sinful, for to be wasteful showed lack of gratitude to the Lord, she advised.

Aunt Lu—because she lived in Houston, and because of my age—accompanied me to the initial endocrinology appointment. I liked the doctor immediately. Due to his entirely bald head, the medical community called him Curly, and the embroidered nickname appeared above the pocket on his white doctor coat. "I could prescribe a medication to shrink the size of the nodule, but given your age and your plans to attend school out of state, I recommend surgery," he said.

"Cissie is going to be a famous movie star one day," Lu said.

"This will result in the loss of half your thyroid—"

"I mean, I don't think you know. You're looking at a future star here," she said.

Dr. Curly nodded. "We find that even with part of the gland missing, the remainder usually picks up the slack and—"

"So it's very important that you don't leave a huge scar on her neck, Doctor."

"And as far as your activity after surgery—"

"She's really quite a singer and dancer."

"It's best if you continue all of your normal activities," he said.

When Lu had enough assurance that he'd opted to use a scalpel, not a hacksaw, on my neck, she moved on to other topics. "My son likes to dissect things. He wants to be a brain surgeon."

My doctor took a few minutes to discuss the ins and outs of the practice of medicine with her. He then booked my surgery, but when I ran the date by Mom, she said it interfered with carpet installation at the new home she and Roy had recently purchased.

"This nodule may or may not be cancerous. We need to take it out immediately, carpet or not," Dr. Curly said.

Mom dug in her heels. "It took me a long time to get this appointment, and I don't want to change it." But after additional urging from my doctor, she rescheduled the installation.

On the morning of the surgery, Dr. Curly came to my hospital room to chat for a few minutes before my transfer to the operating room. He glanced around as if looking for signs of visitors. "Where's your mother?" he asked.

I shrugged. "I don't know."

Chapter Nine

With the surgery behind me, and my first semester at Carnegie Mellon only weeks away, I experienced the priceless feeling that my entire life lay before me, a vast expanse of time that looked promising and kind.

Before I left town, Patsy and I visited Jimmy in the hospital. He'd been admitted for stomach pain, for which the doctors could find no cause. "He's just doing this as an excuse not to work. He's lazy," Dan told me.

Patsy and I sat by Jimmy's bed, our conversation at a standstill as the three of us listened to a woman talking to the elderly patient in a bed several feet away. The partially drawn curtain allowed only the sight of the woman's backside as she leaned over him. Occasionally she would straighten, and I could see her hawklike profile of sharp, jutting bones. "You're inconveniencing so many people," she said. "You always need something. People have to drop what they're doing, all because of you." It would not have surprised me if Dan had stood at Jimmy's bedside, making the same accusations.

The man didn't say a word in his defense. Maybe his illness prevented him from doing so. I wondered if he looked at her as she berated him or if he stared off into space. Maybe he focused on the beautiful trees outside the window. Or the looming storm clouds. It seemed to rain every summer afternoon in Houston for as long as I could remember.

Patsy left the room to report the woman's abuse. "The nurse

said there's nothing she can do about mean family members," she whispered when she returned.

Jimmy couldn't hold down a job, so at some point after his release from the hospital, Dan paid for him to learn piano tuning, then employed him at the music store. The one time I saw him tuning there, he looked so out of place among the older, blind tuners, one of whom Dan fired for asking me to give him my eyes. Day after day, Jimmy existed as one of the annoying square pegs in Dan's life. Not driven or ambitious, but soft-spoken and reserved, he didn't at all take after Dan. He wasn't even musical. When I next saw Jimmy, it was at Dad and Patsy's home. He pulled up in his Toyota, and I ran out to the car and got in. "Wanna drive around and smoke a few cigarettes?" I asked.

His beautiful gray eyes looked sad and tired. "I can't," he said. "It feels like there are bugs crawling all over me. I don't want them to get on you."

I nodded and got out of the car.

I hadn't seen Billy all summer. Toward the end of August, I flew to see him while he participated in the Aspen Music Festival. Mike, his roommate, and I planned it beforehand as a surprise visit. I lied to Mom about where I'd be for a few days. I even told the driver of the cab at the Aspen airport that no one knew where I was. Our eyes met in the rearview mirror. He held my gaze for one moment too long. "You mean no one in the world knows where you are?"

I quickly realized my mistake. "Oh, sure. I mean, his roommate knows I'm on my way."

When Mike and I heard Billy's key in the door, I ran into the bathroom, hopped into the tub, and hid behind the shower curtain. He came into the bathroom and started combing his hair. "Did I get a letter from Sondra today?" he asked Mike.

"No. I didn't see anything from her," he said.

"I don't get it. I haven't heard from her in a week. I wonder what's up."

I peeked out from around the shower curtain. "Hi, Billy," I said. His eyes went wide with surprise. He shut the bathroom door, and we hugged for the longest time.

Students in the festival weren't allowed to have overnight guests in their rooms, so I had to hide the entire time. Mike came and went throughout the day as he participated in various musical events and rehearsals, then slept elsewhere at night. The day before I flew back to Houston, Mike had a major issue with his cello, requiring him to withdraw from the festival. He started packing his things to return home.

Meanwhile, Billy and I ended up in a particularly fervent hours-long make-out session in his bed my last night in Aspen. Finally, at the age of eighteen, the time had come. "Billy, I'm ready," I said.

The door to the room opened. "Sorry, guys. I forgot something," Mike whispered in the dark. Billy rolled off me, and we lay side by side, staring at the ceiling, waiting. Billy and I lost our mojo, so to speak, during the delay but got revved up again a short while after Mike left.

The doorknob turned. "Hey, guys. Sorry. Just one more thing." Billy rolled off me as Mike walked in again. We lay there, growing more resentful by the moment, while Mike puttered around, retrieving this or that. By the time he left the room for the third and final time, it was two in the morning. Frustrated and exhausted, Billy and I gave up. But we'd gotten far enough along, at least technically, to call my virginity a thing of the past.

He got up early to shower the next morning. I remained in bed, wanting to give him his space while he got ready for a rehearsal. There was a knock on the door. Billy came out of the bathroom and looked through the peephole. "It's my dad!" he said. Both of our faces registered horror. Once again, Billy had no warning of his parents' arrival.

I threw the covers off, ran into the bathroom, jumped in the tub, and yanked the curtain a few feet down the rod. Mr. J strode into the room, inserting his influence into Billy's day, asking about his plans, his schedule, his upcoming rehearsals. He then came into the bathroom, put the toilet lid up, and started peeing as he continued his conversation. The shower curtain wasn't closed all the way, and I figured if I could see part of Mr. J, he could see part of me. I remained frozen, pressed against the back of the shower. He zipped up, flushed the toilet, said a few more words to Billy, then left the room. I all but fell out of the shower onto the bathroom floor. It took a good ten minutes before my heart stopped pounding. "What do you think he would have done?" I asked Billy.

"He probably would have thought it was funny," he said. No way in hell did I believe that.

I showered and dressed, packed up, and called a cab to take me to the airport. Billy decided to ride along with me. I later learned that he walked all the way back, and his eyes filled with tears when he saw my plane take off and fly away from him. He missed a rehearsal, and the conductor threatened to kick him out of the festival.

When I returned to Houston, Dan invited me to fly to Las Vegas with him. At some point in the trip, I confided that I'd lost my virginity. My description of the events was animated, and I turned the constant interruptions by Mike into a joke. Dan laughed so hard he had tears in his eyes.

We ran into a friend of his in a casino, and the three of us went to a nearby restaurant for dinner. "She lost her virginity a few days ago," Dan told his friend. "Why don't you tell him about it?" he asked me. I shook my head and stared at my plate.

I looked older than eighteen, and no one questioned my age in Vegas. I played the slots, sat at blackjack tables while Dan played, and drank as much alcohol as I wanted. He took me to R-rated shows, ones with hundreds of topless women. We held hands as we entered so I might appear to be his girlfriend, not his teen stepdaughter.

One afternoon, we stopped off in the hotel gift shop, where he bought *Penthouse* before we returned to our rooms. There was a pass-through door between the two, and I crossed over and sat with him at a small table by the window. He began to share the "Letters" section of the magazine with me. A woman had written in to describe the details of a sexual encounter. "My breast fell out of my robe," Dan read aloud. He pantomimed the woman picking her breast up off the floor and shoving it back into place. I howled with laughter.

He got up and went into the bathroom for a little while. I lay down on his bed, propped myself up on an elbow, and continued to read the letters. Dan returned, wearing only a thin robe. He lay down on the bed, spooned me, and draped his arm over my waist. "Read it to me out loud," he said. His penis and testicles pressed against my butt felt both rubbery and mushy, like soft-boiled eggs, through the silk of his robe.

Eighteen years old, and still unable to tell him no. After reading to him for a while, I got up and went to my room to get ready for dinner.

Chapter Ten

Billy remained at Interlochen for his senior year. I started classes at Carnegie Mellon. After an out-of-town audition, he changed his flight reservations and flew to Pittsburgh to spend the night with me instead of returning to school immediately. Billy said his father found out and flew into a rage on the phone.

One of the weekends I visited him at Interlochen coincided with his senior concerto concert. After checking in at the campus hotel, I headed toward his dorm. I saw Mr. J walking in his determined way past the main concourse. Billy hadn't thought to warn me, having adjusted to his parents' frequent and unannounced appearances in his life. But how foolish of me not to have foreseen their presence that weekend. I greeted them with a forced smile over the next few days.

The day before my return to CMU, Billy and I agreed to meet in his room after his classes, hang out for a while, then have dinner together in the cafeteria. When I crossed through the hotel lobby, Mr. J exited in front of me, looking as if he were in a great hurry, and headed off in the direction of Billy's dorm. Mrs. Stein—the mother of two IAA students—blocked my way. She and Mr. and Mrs. J had become close friends over the years through campus visits, parent weekends, and concerts. "Sit down, Sondra. I want to talk with you."

"I can't. I'm going to meet Billy."

"Sit down. This will only take a minute."

I sat on a sofa in the lobby, turned to face her, and remained on the edge of the couch cushion, poised for a quick getaway. For about twenty minutes, Mrs. Stein droned on about no particular subject. I nodded yes, or shook my head when it seemed appropriate, but remained confused about her stream-of-consciousness lecture and why she felt such urgency to talk to me. We'd never said more than a few words to each other over the years. "Do you know how the French pronounce pointe?" she asked.

"No," I said.

"They pronounce it *pwont*."

I nodded and wondered if my heavy coat hid my impatient sighs. She continued a monologue about subjects that seemed to have no relation to one another. When Mr. J strode into the lobby, I quickly rose, said goodbye, and headed off to meet Billy.

"Yes, she is sick," I overheard her say to Mr. J. "She's sick."

I sat by an open window in my hotel room that afternoon, smoking a cigarette. I heard a door open and close, then Billy's voice. I hadn't known until then that Mr. and Mrs. J occupied the room next to mine. I sighed and shook my head.

"Mrs. Stein talked to Sondra this afternoon and said she's sick," Mr. J said.

"What are you talking about?" Billy asked.

"I'm telling you she's sick. That's a sick girl you're dating, son. I should know."

Ouch. Mr. J worked as an optometrist at the state mental hospital in Missouri. I quickly put out my cigarette, afraid that if too much smoke went into their room, they might shut the window, leaving me unable to hear.

"But you don't understand," Billy said. "We're good together. We talk a lot and—"

"Well, good! You talk a lot!" Mr. J said.

Mrs. J offered only one comment, spoken too softly for me to hear.

"That girl's got expensive taste too. You're never going to be able to support her," Mr. J said. His lecture abruptly ended. Succinct and brutal. Billy left their room.

The earlier events in the hotel lobby slowly came together. Mr. J had rushed off to detain Billy in his dorm room to provide Mrs. Stein enough time to render judgment. After overhearing her pronouncement about my mental health, I'd assumed her to be a professional therapist or counselor; otherwise, why would Mr. J place any value on her opinion? But no. I later learned that she taught dance at a small college.

My flight back to Pittsburgh left the next morning. During a layover at O'Hare, I decided to call Mom from a pay phone in an airport restaurant. She answered almost immediately, and I tearfully poured out the conversation I'd overheard. "He said I'm sick! And then he said Billy could never support me."

"Well, maybe he's right," Mom said. "You know, musicians don't make that much money."

"Whatever. Bye, Mom."

At CMU, musical theater majors attended class from nine in the morning until five in the afternoon, and when the "dramats"—the nickname for drama majors—performed, we returned at six to work the sets, comb wigs, do laundry, rehang costumes, and do any other necessary grunt work. After I'd worked *Madwoman of Chaillot* until after midnight one evening, I missed classes the next day due to two pulled muscles in my back and a urinary tract infection. I'd never experienced the horrific discomfort of a UTI, and the infection proved so severe, I could see blood in my pee. I made it to the clinic for a prescription but could not attend classes that day. Instead of running down the dorm hallway to the bathroom every few minutes, I camped out on the toilet.

The next day, I passed a drama major in the hallway of the administrative building. "Eysselinck's considering kicking you out of the department for missing class," he said.

Walter Eysselinck was the department head, and his office was only several feet down the hallway. I walked in, approached the receptionist, and asked to see him.

"It's fine," a voice to my left said. "Come on in."

I'd never met the man. The wide face held the most piercing eyes, almost mesmerizing, in a shade of blue I'd never seen. He looked at me expectantly and rather kindly. Until I told him my name. His expression changed to pouty, righteous indignation, and his eyes flashed anger. More anger than I felt I deserved for missing a few classes. Then again, as the head of the department, and as an actor himself, he'd obviously mastered the art of conveying abrupt shifts in emotion. Details of the UTI and my bladder's constant demands for immediate access to a toilet caused him to visibly blanch. "And yes, I went to the campus clinic. If you don't believe me, you can call them." He quickly excused my absence and directed me out of his office.

Then, dance class the next morning. "Where were you yesterday? We missed you," the teacher called out to me.

"I was sick."

"Dancers do not get sick!" he announced to the class.

I proved to be an equal-opportunity offender of faculty. I had no talent for sight singing. This so frustrated my music theory teacher, who never pronounced my name correctly, that she once slammed a folder down on the piano when I failed to properly sing a stanza of music. "Damn it, Sandra! Stop wasting the class's time!" She then labeled me an underachiever in front of the class. If I did manage to perform correctly, she praised me as if I were a puppy that had finally hit the paper. "Yes, yes! That is so good, Sandra. So good, yes!"

Drama and musical theater majors spent several hours a week in Voice and Speech class. We blew air through our lips like a horse. We emitted huge sighs as we repeatedly bent from the waist and let our bodies go limp. We brought our bodies upright with a slow, ascending "Whooooop!" We learned the difference between shallow and deep breathing—as if it were not intuitively obvious—and even how to stand from the prone position most efficiently. Or we imitated zoo animals. We tried not to laugh, or groan, when our teacher instructed us to close our eyes and imagine ourselves naked in a bathtub of crushed peaches while chanting, "Peachy, peachy, peachy. Yummy, yummy, yummy." A few of us believed our teacher did sit naked in a tub of peaches from time to time.

Desperate, I called Mom. "I have to get out of here. I don't know how much longer I can last."

"But why?" she asked. "We just got your midterm report card. Roy is so proud. You got almost straight As!"

Roy had mistakenly read the Class Section column instead of the grades. The musical theater department offered only one class in most of the subjects, which received the section designation of A. I had section F for history, but also failed the class. Not only had I never attended, I'd never bothered to officially drop the class. Mom said she didn't have the heart to tell Roy, who had shown my report card to almost everyone who came to the house. She begged me to hold out a little while longer. I did, but even sedating myself with beer and pot every night couldn't keep me there. I left CMU for good at the end of the semester. On the way back to Texas, I auditioned in New York for the Alvin Ailey Dance Company. They offered me a summer scholarship, scheduled to begin in June.

As Roy and I sat at the breakfast table together the morning after my arrival, we discussed my university plans, which, at that point, proved pretty much nonexistent. He said he didn't know why I'd felt the need to attend a school clear across the country anyway. "If ya cain't find what yer lookin' for in Texas, it doesn't exist."

"Okay."

"Go to school a couple of years. Find yerself a husband."

"Yeah, well, you were right about CMU, anyway," I said.

"That's a fine quality you got there . . . admittin' when yer wrong." Hearing this admission from me put our relationship on an entirely new course. Maybe all along, he'd wanted to know I didn't hate him. And he helped me develop a plan. Next stop: University of Texas at Austin.

Before beginning classes, I called Dad in Houston to see if I'd left some posters at his house the previous summer. Patsy answered the phone with a weak and raspy voice. "My god," I said. "Are you sick?"

"No, I'm not sick," she said, sounding annoyed. Her voice softened. "We've had a terrible thing happen in our family, honey. Jimmy's dead."

I'd heard little about him since visiting him in the hospital, except for an occasional comment about possible drug use and his involvement with the Jehovah's Witnesses. At the age of twenty-two, he'd recently returned to live with Dad and Patsy. She'd come home from work a few days before and found a note he'd left by the phone. It told her where to find his body.

The bridge had raised expansion joints that caused a constant and deafening vibration as thousands of cars passed over them every day. If anyone heard Jimmy fire the gun, they probably attributed the noise to bridge traffic or a backfiring car. His body lay undiscovered until Patsy found him late that afternoon.

After the funeral, I started classes at UT-Austin, majoring in Spanish and minoring in English literature. I took a jazz class to stay in some semblance of dancing shape. The teacher taught us choreography to a Ray Charles song, and we worked that one piece, three times a week, every week, for the entire semester.

The people, the city, and the campus felt safe. Musicians performed on the main drag by the campus, at bars, on sidewalks, in music halls, everywhere. We blasted Fleetwood Mac, Foreigner, Jackson Browne, and Boston on our car radios and dorm stereos. The smell of pot wafted through the hallways. Scenic, uncrowded, cultural, and liberal, Austin also offered sunny weather, and the spring and summer heat made hanging out much more enticing than attending classes. Regardless, I loved my core courses and excelled in them with little effort. I'd never been happier. But during my walks to and from class, my thoughts at times turned pensive, and memories of Dan surfaced.

I am five years old. Dan sits on the couch, and I stand in front of him, naked. To his side, there's a small stack of bathing suits he wants me to try on. I step into one of them and find there's no real top to it, just crisscrosses of fabric that don't adequately cover my nipples. "No! No! No!" I yell. Mom looks out from the kitchen and smiles.

Dan laughs and pulls the bathing suit down to my ankles. I hold his shoulders for balance and step out. He takes another from the stack and has me try it on.

I am eight or nine years old. I dance naked in the bathroom one night while waiting for the tub to fill. The steps are particularly stupid—showgirl-type moves, with lots of bouncing and kicking. I catch a sliver of Mom's reflection at the far side of the mirror as she stands in the hallway watching me through the crack in the barely open door. I quickly shut the door just as Dan steps over to peek in at me.

I reminded myself how often Dan had said he loved me. But if his touch and his eyes upon my naked little-girl body had been natural, normal, and loving, why had I felt such embarrassment and agitation? *No, no, no. He loved me; he always said he did. I'm overthinking this . . . reading too much into things.* I had no satisfactory answers and filed these confusing memories away, refusing to let him intrude on my newfound happiness. *Besides, Dan was always right.*

A dance major introduced me to a friend of hers who lived in the same dorm, and he and I went out to dinner. A touch too shy for my liking, but easy enough to be around. We spent more time with one another, such as eating meals together in the cafeteria. He invited me to spend a weekend at home with him in rice-farming country down by the Gulf. His mother proved hypervigilant about our being alone in any of the bedrooms, and when she had to be out of the house, his younger sister stepped in to stand guard. She patrolled the hallways and scolded him if she found him in the guest room with me. She and the mother were captivated by a television show one night, and he and I managed to have sex in his bedroom. As far as my new sex life, it was like I'd gotten a bicycle and wanted to ride it. Often. When we returned to the dorm the following Monday, he moved into my room.

I'd been away from Billy for months and had seen him only three times since my graduation from Interlochen. He planned to attend Northwestern in Illinois in the fall, and I, happy as a clam at high tide in Austin, planned to remain in Texas. I flew to Michigan and told him that the thousand-mile distance between us proved unworkable. "I've met someone else," I said.

"Did you sleep with him?" Billy asked.

"Yes," I said.

He put his hands over his face and turned away from me. I waited through the long silence. "It must have been so hard for you to come all this way to tell me. Thank you. Thank you for telling me in person."

The semester ended in the first part of June, and I flew to New York to start the Alvin Ailey summer dance scholarship, for which I'd auditioned after leaving Carnegie Mellon. Mom gave me a check for $200 before I left. After making the first rent payment at the Barbizon Hotel, I had little money and frequently ate microwaved popcorn for lunch and dinner.

Along with jazz classes, the curriculum required a ballet class. The first day, we spent twenty minutes learning how to properly do a demi-plié, the most basic part of a warm-up at the barre and one of the very first movements likely executed when beginning the study of ballet. The dance curriculum bored me. I found the city crowded, smoggy, humid, and hot. When I looked up, I saw only small squares of hazy sky instead of the big, open expanses of blue I'd grown accustomed to in Texas. I could stretch my arms out, aim my face at the sun, and breathe in Texas. New Yorkers struck me as closed off—reluctant to engage past a bare minimum. I felt inconsequential and in the way.

Late one afternoon after classes, I wandered into a bookstore near my hotel, a business I'd passed a few times a day on my way back and forth to dance classes but had never entered. I had no money to spare but decided to browse books to pass some time. A man stepped out from behind the checkout counter, approached me, and struck up a conversation that at first involved a few minutes of small talk, then turned alarming. "I had you followed," he said.

"What? What did you say?"

"I saw you walking past a few times, so I asked one of my employees to follow you to see where you go every day."

I left the bookstore and went up to my hotel room. Creeped out, lonely, bored, and disillusioned, I decided to leave New York. I called Mom for help getting a plane ticket and flew to Houston. My boyfriend had returned home for the summer, to the tiny town on the outskirts of Houston where he grew up, and he'd started a job at the Gulf Oil refinery on Interstate 10. I convinced him to get an apartment with me, and I found an inexpensive one with a month-to-month lease in one of the worst sections of Houston. We moved in together, and he supported us with his salary. While he worked that summer, I did nothing but watch soap operas all day and only left the apartment to go to the grocery store. The emptiness of my days brought a sort of contentment. No more rehearsals, lines to learn, competitions, auditions, nothing. A break that felt permanent. Although relieved, without the fine arts I struggled to define myself. If not a singer, what? If not a dancer, who?

When summer ended and my boyfriend and I returned to school, I lived with him and a friend of his in an apartment fifteen minutes or so from campus. I skipped school too often and earned mediocre grades. The school year passed pleasantly enough. My boyfriend returned home for the summer, and I remained in Austin and shared an apartment with my brother while I took a history course at the community college. On the day of the final, Austin had severe flash flooding, and I chose to stay home. I never bothered to contact the teacher to make up the exam and earned an incomplete for the course.

Fall semester, I rented an apartment near campus and invited my boyfriend to move in with me and my Chihuahua, Carmen, which I'd adopted from the pound over the summer. Up to that point, he'd fulfilled my desire for a calm, undemanding male, but after months of watching pot increasingly rob him of all motivation, his extreme passivity began to grate on my nerves. After a while, I could only see faults. He spent much of his time skipping classes and getting high. He'd even set up fluorescent lights in my closet to nurture the pot plants he attempted to grow. I grew impatient and snappish with him and imagined myself using a cattle prod on his ass, the ass that did little but sit on my couch all day.

Every single morning, he fussed over his hair and tried to tame the feathered layers with an inordinate amount of Final Net hairspray, which not only deposited a film on my contact lenses but twice set off migraines so severe that I vomited. His mother didn't want him to work while in school but only sent him $100 a month, a portion of which he dedicated to pot purchases, leaving little to contribute to our expenses. He revealed one morning that he'd had sex with me while I was asleep. "You were on your side," he said. "I just pressed up against you and went on in," he said. I could remember none of it and felt disgust and violation. The frequent sight of him sitting on the toilet, his jeans around his ankles and either his finger up his nose or his bong pressed to his mouth, repulsed me. A pharmacy major, he'd already failed organic chemistry twice by rarely going to class and only studying for exams the night before. Around my family, he was inordinately shy, so much so that he struggled to participate in conversations. My relatives intimidated him, and perhaps deservedly so, as he didn't even know how to properly hold a wine glass. "They're just so . . . so . . . I don't know," he said after we had lunch with several of them at a Houston restaurant. "I had to picture each of them sitting on the toilet, to make them, like, more human."

A pot-smoking buddy of his who lived a few doors down from us in the apartment complex put him in touch with contacts who agreed to sell him a large quantity of pot. "I'm driving to Mexico to get it. You wanna go with me?" my boyfriend asked.

A long car ride sounded nice. "Okay. Sure. I'll go." On the designated night, I grabbed a pillow for my lap for Carmen, and the three of us set off for Mexico. At the border, an officer gave us a cursory glance and waved us through. We easily found the home of the dealers, and Carmen and I waited in the den and talked to a chatty guy who looked to be about my age and whose general appearance differed little from most college students I knew. My boyfriend and I went out to the car about twenty minutes later, and I watched him load six Hefty garbage bags of pot into the trunk.

We pulled up to the United States entry point, where an officer waved our car forward to a thick line painted on the concrete, then motioned with his palm for us to stop. The lighting in the area was operating-room bright, so bright it simulated daylight, even though we'd arrived past ten o'clock. The officer leaned down to the driver's side window. "What's your business in Mexico?" he asked.

"We were just visiting friends," my boyfriend mumbled.

The officer shone his flashlight on my face, then let the beam rest on Carmen, asleep on the pillow on my lap. He straightened and took a step back. "You can go," he said.

The long arm of the gate in front of us raised to allow us through. I waited. I looked over at my boyfriend, who made no move to put the car in drive. "Go," I said, quietly. He looked at me, back at the officer, then back at me.

"You can go," the officer said, louder this time. The officer frowned and acted a bit twitchy, raising his eyebrows and leaning forward to study the demeanor of my frozen boyfriend. He stepped back toward the car.

"I can go?" my boyfriend asked him.

"He said you can go!" I said. We drove through the gate and into the United States. "Jesus Christ, what was your problem?" I asked.

"Guess I was just nervous. I dunno."

We passed the next hour or so relieved, tired, and focused on the dark, unlit road. The beams of the headlights created a hypnotic array of shadows in the darkness. When we crossed a small bridge, the shadows turned into flickering hues of aqua and rose. A police car appeared behind us with blue and red lights flashing. My boyfriend pulled to the side of the road, stopped, and rolled down the window. An officer appeared, leaned over, and shone his flashlight throughout the interior of the car. Carmen awoke but did not bark at him. "Do you know why I stopped you?" the officer asked.

"No, I don't," my boyfriend said.

"You been drinking?"

My boyfriend shook his head. "No, officer."

"You were weaving out of your lane when you crossed that bridge."

"Sorry, officer. Guess I'm just tired."

"Where you two headed?"

"Just back to Austin. We go to school there."

The officer was quiet for a few moments. "All right, then," he said, with a pat to the top of the car door. "Try to be a little more careful."

We made it back to the apartment late that night with no further encounters with the law. The next day, I watched as my boyfriend weighed pot and put it into baggie after baggie, making "lids" he planned to sell for $10 each. No longer a recreational user, but a dealer. A pharmacy major no less. I'd dedicated myself to a passive, unmotivated guy who risked flunking out of school entirely when smoking pot became his major. I'd lost all attraction to him. No more screwing around, I told myself. I had my own future to think about. I applied for a part-time position at Austin National Bank and got it on the spot. A few days later, I told the boyfriend to leave my apartment and my life.

He moved in with another pot buddy, one who lived about a mile away, and made a habit of showing up unexpectedly at my front door, as if we might simply pick up where we left off. But I had classes to attend and a job, leaving little time to trifle with his unannounced appearances. The last time I let him in was a workday, and I'd gotten home from school only a few minutes before. "I have to change clothes for work," I said over my shoulder as he followed me into the bedroom.

"I can't forget what you look like without your clothes on," he said.

As I pulled together what I planned to wear, I started humming a song I heard frequently on the radio while driving to work. "It's not the meat, it's the motion . . . ," I sang as I started to get dressed.

He looked at me with disgust. "I can't believe you'd sing that!"

"What's the big deal with what I sang?"

"The words. You're not even the same person. You're—"

I turned and strode toward him. "You know what? You're not my boyfriend anymore, and I don't care what you think."

His jaw tensed and his eyes narrowed. "I could punch you out right now," he said, making a fist.

"Do it!" I said. When he didn't swing, I stepped closer. "Go ahead and do it!"

His arm tensed and his fist tightened. I waited and held his gaze. I had no doubt that this always high, always unmotivated, always passive male would *not* hit me. He shook his head, turned away, and left my apartment.

Chapter Eleven

After a week or so at the bank, my boss, Beth, walked over to me in the cafeteria with a handsome young man in tow. His feathered hairstyle formed a perfect helmet, exactly like John Travolta in *Saturday Night Fever*. "Sondra, this is my friend Kyle. Kyle, Sondra."

"Sandra?" he said, with raised eyebrows.

"Sondra," I said.

"Sonia?" he said.

Beth rolled her eyes and shook her head.

"Sondra," I said.

"Oh! So your name is Sondra!" he said, sounding as if he'd unraveled a great mystery.

Yeah. That's what I said.

A few days later, he called down to the basement, where we processed the check orders and printing. "Hey, a lot of us are going dancing this Friday night. You wanna go?"

"Sure! Sounds great," I said.

Later in the week, he called again. "Everyone else canceled. Looks like it'll just be you and me. Still wanna go?"

"That's fine," I said.

Friday afternoon, he called again. "Instead of going out tonight, I think I'm gonna stay home and work on my motorcycle."

"Oh. Hmmm," I said. "Well, bye then."

I turned to Beth, whose desk was behind mine. "Kyle said he'd rather work on his motorcycle than go out tonight."

She rolled her eyes, said nothing, then got up and left the office. I found out later that she'd gone up to his office and lectured him about his stupidity.

About ten minutes later, Kyle called. "Okay, I guess we could go ahead and go out. I mean if you still want to," he said.

Still processing coming in second place to a motorcycle, my ego arose and cried out in my defense. *I must make myself attractive to this man. I must make him like me.* "Yeah, sure," I said. We went country-western dancing that night and had a bang-up time. Tall, long-legged, with an athletic physique, and good god could he dance. He taught me some swing and earned major points for being one of the few men I'd met who could teach me something new about dancing.

After our next date, at a dinner theater, I invited him up to my apartment to play backgammon. We played for hours. He often spoke to my two goldfish, Piggly and Wiggly, who swam back and forth, watching us through the side of their glass bowl. "Pig. Wig. She's beatin' the pants off me here." He eventually made his way over to my side of the coffee table, and we kissed for a few minutes. "So, do I get to stay the night?" he asked.

"No," I said.

"Why?"

"Because I hardly know you," I said.

He looked confused but let it go at that. "Can I see you again?" he asked.

"Yes," I said.

The ex-boyfriend apparently kept a close eye on my comings and goings while hanging out frequently with a pot buddy a few doors down from my apartment. I came home from class one afternoon and found WHORE written in black magic marker on my front door. I turned around and went to the manager's office at the end of the parking lot. "My ex wrote on my door. Could you maybe . . ."

He smiled sympathetically and nodded, as if he fully understood the workings of the spurned-male mind. "I'll get someone up there right away," he said.

Kyle went to his car early one morning after spending the night with me and found the air let out of one of his tires. A few days later, my car wouldn't start. Although excellent with car and motorcycle mechanics, Kyle couldn't determine what the problem might be and called a tow for me. The driver got out of his truck and met us over by my car. "Looks like somebody's mad, Miss," he said, pointing. "Somebody" had carved WHORE into the paint over the rear wheel well.

When I responded one day to a pounding on my apartment door, I peeked through the curtains and saw no one there. When I opened the door, I found a slab of raw meat on my welcome mat. I left it there. A few hours later, it was gone.

Two months after my first date with Kyle, he and I lay naked and face down at the end of my bed one morning, with our coffee cups on the carpet in front of us. He entertained me with his imitation of a gap-toothed English actor from a film I'd never seen, telling me the plot and reciting lines with an English accent tinged with a southern drawl. When my laughter died out, he grew silent, then turned on his side to face me. "What do you think about marrying me?"

"When would you want to do this?" I asked, sounding like a receptionist booking his dental procedure.

"How about toward the end of the summer?"

I stared out the window for a few moments and shrugged. "Okay," I said.

Several days later, we drove to Mom and Roy's house to tell

them in person. We planned to talk to them the next morning over breakfast, but Roy left unexpectedly to see a racehorse he wanted to buy. This left Mom to deal with the situation entirely by herself. "Oh, god. I wish Roy was here," she said over and over. "Cissie, just wait. Wait till you finish school. What's the rush?"

But I saw no reason to take advice from a woman already in her fourth marriage. Why should I wait? Handsome, funny, ambitious, and a good dancer—I knew of nothing else to want in a husband. After a few minutes of her pleading, interspersed with frequent "God, I wish Roy would come home," I burst into tears and ran out of the kitchen. Kyle told me later that she wasted no words. "I know when my daughter's bein' taken advantage of," she said. "She just got out of a relationship. What is it you want?"

"Well, that went about like I thought it would," Kyle said as we pulled out of the driveway and headed back to Austin.

Roy called that evening. "Honey, your mother told me about your plans. If you wanna get married, you get married. We'll support your decision." Mom flew in a few days later, and we spent three days booking the church, making reception arrangements at a hotel, choosing my china and silver patterns, setting up the wedding registry, hiring a photographer, and ordering flowers. She hired a wedding planner to handle the rest.

Kyle's parents welcomed me with open arms. They were heavy drinkers and gave us a bottle of tequila and a blender as a wedding gift, which in my view only added to their novelty as in-laws. Surely, marrying a man with such an accepting, entertaining family could only further enhance my happy life. After the wedding, Kyle and I drove with Carmen to his parents' home in Houston. They'd agreed to care for her while we honeymooned in Ixtapa-Zihuatanejo. My mother-in-law, who grew up in Sao Paulo, Brazil, told us that if we needed help or a special favor while in Mexico to remember that Latinos love romance. "Tell them, '*Somos novidades*,'" she instructed. "You're telling them you're newlyweds. They'll love that." I had no honeymoon vocabulary in my knowledge of Spanish and appreciated the tip.

The next morning, only hours before our flight, I awoke to both sides of my lower jaw in a full-throb ache. My in-laws rushed me to their family dentist, who determined that my wisdom teeth had chosen that day for their attempt to emerge through the gums. I left his office with a prescription for a painkiller.

My new in-laws, inveterate travelers, gave us pills to prevent intestinal upset from the water in Mexico, and per their instructions, we'd started taking them the previous day. By the end of the first day of our honeymoon, the only conversation Kyle wanted to engage in concerned his digestion. He'd become uncomfortable, sweaty, and grouchy. The meds not only prevented him from having diarrhea but prevented him from pooping at all. I had no problems with the anti-diarrhea pills and quite enjoyed my pain meds. My newlywed sex drive revved in high gear, but Kyle claimed his blocked bowels killed any desire.

Ixtapa-Zihuatanejo had a definite tourist season, but when we honeymooned there at the end of August, we'd missed it, and there were few visitors due to the sweltering heat. Kyle complained to the front desk that our hotel room had no air-conditioning. "*Novidades*," Kyle said, pointing back and forth between us.

The desk clerk responded with a strained smile. "Ocean air. Room cool from ocean," he said.

Most shops had closed weeks before, and restaurants had few choices. "It's out of season," our waiters often replied to our requests.

"Oh, okay. What about this?" I'd ask, requesting a different entrée.

"Out of season."

"So, like, what's left? *Somos novidades*," Kyle said, pointing back and forth between the two of us. The waiter frowned and shook his head.

Kyle could only take a few bites of food at each meal, saying anything he ate stalled somewhere within his body and refused to move, but we continued to go to restaurants for something to do. We sat on the beach the rest of the time. "I can't believe you're tanning so fast," he said.

I got caught in an undertow while he tried to teach me how to bodysurf. I regained my footing away from him and stumbled toward the shore, the waves knocking me off my feet. My waist-length hair had flipped over my head and plastered itself over my nose and mouth, preventing me from breathing. I stopped, gasping for air, and pushed the sopping mass out of my face. I trudged over the sand and dropped down onto my towel, exhausted. While I coughed and tried to catch my breath, Kyle came out of the water and plopped down beside me. "Wow. I thought you were a goner there for a second," he said. He looked at my legs again. "I can't believe you're tanning faster than me."

Day three of the honeymoon: Still no poop, still no sex. He thought it was great fun that evening to chase me around the hotel room and squirt his contact lens saline solution at me. He cornered me and shot a full stream into my face. When I cried out for him to stop, he squirted it in my mouth. The next morning, in the hotel coffee shop, I burst into tears. "Do you want to call off the marriage?" he asked quietly.

I stared at my lap. Roy had spent so much on the wedding. I'd have to return countless gifts. I'd be forced to admit my marriage couldn't even last four days. Above all, I could not, would not, openly acknowledge that maybe Mom had been right. "No," I said.

That night, Kyle came out of the bathroom and announced that he'd finally pooped. We had sex, but I found no comfort or consolation in it. By then, I only wanted to go home.

As we waited at the gate for our flight the next morning, a woman sitting across from us opened a newspaper and started to read. At the top of the first page a bold title read NOVIDADES. "That's weird," I said. "Do they print marriages in the newspapers here?"

"Dunno," Kyle said, shrugging.

I reached into our travel bag, pulled out my Spanish-English dictionary, and found the word. "Great," I said. "We told all those people we were daily news."

Chapter Twelve

On our first night home, I looked around at the new apartment we'd moved into two weeks before the wedding. We had jobs to return to on Monday, bills coming due, and hardly any furniture, and my car needed extensive work. *So, this is what it feels like to be an adult.* We had no dining room table, so we ate dinner with our plates balanced on our laps while watching television. I took our dishes into the kitchen and came back to our borrowed couch. When I scooted over by Kyle to snuggle, he feigned an exaggerated squirm and nudged me away with his shoulder. "I don't like that. It makes me feel boxed in." I moved over to "my side" of the couch and from then on respected the imaginary line that separated us.

Although he'd promised Mom I could stay in school, he decided we couldn't afford the tuition, or afford much else, so I went to work full-time. Due to the bank's nepotism policy, which stated that as a married couple we could not work in the same building, I accepted a transfer to open new accounts for a start-up branch. Mind-numbing tedium. I mostly sat at my desk and watched the passing cars on the highway, wondering how life could so abruptly change into something so colorless. If I'd had anything to look forward to at home at the end of the day, anything more than my Chihuahua, I might have more easily coped. But sitting next to Kyle on the couch was off-limits, asking him to run errands with me proved pointless, and wanting sex every day made him feel smothered. "I am not a machine!" he'd yelled at me.

Desperate for emotional and sexual connection, I stayed up late waiting for him to tire of television, or I lay awake in bed hoping to seduce him before he fell asleep. It led to my being so sleep-deprived, I could hardly get out of bed in the morning. On the rare occasions he deigned to have sex, his touch was rushed and mechanical. I often cried afterward, knowing our next encounter might be weeks away.

Surely our problems had to be my fault. I had to give him more physical and emotional space; I could accept that maybe frequent shows of affection weren't his thing. And I truly did lack cooking skills. He labeled my first attempt at making Cream of Wheat as "The Lumps of Wheat Breakfast." I wondered if he didn't find me attractive enough. Maybe he preferred another type of woman. He obviously needed me to do or be *something* different but did not voice it. I switched into high gear on all counts. When he came home from work at night, he always walked into an immaculate apartment. I'd fixed my hair and makeup and greeted him in a negligee. A hot meal awaited him. Nothing I tried made a difference. He dropped his briefcase at the door, asked about dinner, then spent the remainder of the evening watching television.

As soon as we'd said "I do," I felt as if he viewed sex with me as one of life's unpleasant but necessary chores. If I were at all vocal during sex, his hand over my mouth silenced me. Any discussion of sex added to a powder keg of pressure and avoidance within him, and my desperate need for connection further pushed him away. After a year of only having sex a handful of times, my confusion and frustration reached a boiling point one night after coming home from work. He'd already made himself at home on the couch, fully settled in for hours of sitcoms. I don't recall what specifically set off the argument, but my emotions increasingly roiled, primed for explosion. I burst into tears, pulled off my high-heeled shoes, and hurled them against the wall above the television I'd grown to hate. "I can't do this! Why can't we have sex? We're supposed to have sex! What the fuck is wrong?" I yelled.

Seated on the couch, not looking me in the eye, he remained quiet for a while, appearing to choose his words carefully. "Sondra, it takes you too long to come."

My anger and humiliation were so all-encompassing, my desire for him dissolved in a heartbeat. Of all the perceived personal failings I'd blamed for the tension in our relationship, I'd never once considered that any facet of my strong sexual attraction to him was the cause of the serious problems in our marriage. But instead of summoning the courage to run like a woman possessed and file for divorce, I inwardly declared war. If he didn't want me sexually, then I vowed to want him even less. From then on, I had my nose in a book when at home. I didn't stay up until all hours waiting for him to tire of television. When I went to bed, I went to sleep. It had hurt too much to want sex from him. I made sure I no longer did.

Any information gleaned about the inner workings of Kyle's mind revealed itself indirectly. His parents visited us once during the first year of our marriage, and the three of us sat in the bleachers together to watch him pitch a nighttime softball game. The stakes were high for making the playoffs. We had to beat the Austin Police Department—not only excellent softball players but well known by our team for having a heckler from hell. We'd lost against APD previously, but not embarrassingly so, and had fared somewhat well against the heckler, a man with long, scraggly gray hair, dirty jeans, and a booming voice.

He stood ready and waiting when Kyle stepped onto the pitcher's mound, and kept himself in his line of sight behind the home-base referee. "You couldn't hit the side of a barn!" Heckler yelled.

Kyle appeared calm. He pitched. "Ball one!" the ref called.

"Here's Ty Cobb!" Kyle's father yelled.

Heckler broke out into exaggeratedly loud laughter. "You call that pitching?"

Kyle repositioned himself and pitched again. "Ball two!" said the ref.

"My grandmother can pitch better than that!" Heckler called out.

Kyle walked another batter. And another. Another. "You gotta be kidding me!" Heckler yelled. The APD team grew more raucous. Their whoops, applause, and laughter swelled each time Kyle walked another batter. His pitching remained so erratic, the other team scored points by doing little more than stepping into the batter's box and waiting. "Don't even try, pitcher! What's the use?" Heckler called out, beside himself with joy. For a split second, I thought of coming down from the bleachers and quietly begging the man to stop. But I stayed where I was.

Our team maintained their positions but no longer stood tensed and ready to field balls. Their stances relaxed, and a few even stood with a hand on a hip, waiting. Finally, after walking fifteen batters, Kyle ran over to the shortstop and said a few words. He took off his glove, and the teammate, who had little or no experience as a pitcher, took over.

We lost by an overwhelming margin. After the game, Kyle couldn't get to the car fast enough. When the two of us walked into the apartment, he dropped down onto the couch. He sat with his elbow on the armrest, his face hidden in his hand. Silent. Then he started to cry. I moved toward him from my side of the couch, but he extended his palm toward me. "It's okay, it's okay," he said. The distance between us only allowed me to stroke his shoulder. "My dad. My dad. Tonight of all nights." He began to sob. "I wanted to prove to him I'm good at something." I inched closer and tried to put my arm around him. "It's fine. I'm fine," he said, shrugging me off.

He wiped the tears from his face and composed himself. The small window of vulnerability he'd allowed me to see closed.

Chapter Thirteen

After we paid for the repairs on my car, Kyle decided we couldn't afford to keep it. He controlled the money and the checkbook, and instead of purchasing another car for me, he insisted that we could not afford to own two cars. I'd accepted a new job as a receptionist at an office close to his, so he and I rode to work together every day. No longer in school, and with no easy access to friends I'd made through classes or prior jobs, I'd become more and more isolated. When my workday grew quiet, I'd stare out the front window and wonder how, at the age of twenty-two, I could already feel like a dried-up old woman. I'd traded college, my own apartment, my car, and my personal and financial freedom to be the wife of a man I seemed only to annoy. And yet, I never considered the possibility of taking the necessary actions to get my old life back. I saw no possible way to effect a reset, so I plodded on through the days, always carrying the ache of rejection.

Almost every conversation with Mom included mention of Kyle's broken promise that I'd stay in school, and I continued to make excuses for him. We had only one car. We both had full-time jobs but lived paycheck to paycheck. Even I saw no possible way to afford the tuition or work out the logistics of transportation. Roy, who placed value on a college education like no one I'd ever known, stepped in. He offered to move us to the small town where he and Mom lived, help us find a place to rent, and provide an interest-free loan to get us through the first year of school. Kyle and I never discussed whether we'd accept his offer. Of course we accepted.

Kyle had flunked out of UT-Austin a couple of years before I met him. Skipping a few classes here and there his sophomore year started harmlessly enough, then increased to the point of missing assignments and tests, then snowballed to falling hopelessly behind, culminating in the sickening realization that no amount of work could possibly save his grades. He'd stopped going to classes altogether and remained at the frat house all day watching television. His fraternity brothers came and went, shaking their heads at him camped out in the den, and finally stopped asking questions. When his overall GPA fell to 1.72, his father issued an ultimatum. "You can live here at home and attend University of Houston, or else you're on your own."

"Well, I guess I'm on my own then," Kyle replied, and soon started working at the bank where we met. He later admitted that seeing me doing homework reminded him of his failure. My efforts in college had gnawed at him.

Roy initially lent us a couple thousand dollars for the move, tuition, and books. Kyle and I got part-time jobs, and I joined the local civic ballet. We rented a house almost walking distance from Mom and Roy but didn't see them often. I'd always had the impression that their marriage clicked along well enough, but Mom soon confided that they argued more often. Sodden in alcohol and pills, Roy lost track of time. "He claims I'm never home anymore. He says I never cook for him, but it seems like all I *do* is cook for him," she said, rolling her eyes.

For about six weeks, Mom made excuses for why she couldn't see me. Work, school, and the ballet company gave me little time to be overly concerned. On the day she finally allowed me to visit, she let me in, then pulled out an extra-large envelope from the closet by the front door. "I want you to see this," she said. She held up an X-ray and positioned it to be backlit by the sun coming in through a nearby window. I easily made out a lower leg and foot. "This is the fracture," she said, running her finger down a thin line on the shinbone. "Roy and I got into an argument, and he kicked me. I didn't want you to see me in a cast."

One evening, several months later, she called me in tears. "Can you get over here immediately?" I found her in the kitchen, with spots of what looked like blood on the front of her blouse. From what I could tell, Roy wasn't home. She looked scared and wide-eyed with disbelief. "He got mad, grabbed me by the hair, and slammed my face down in the steaks," she said, pointing to the thawing meat on the counter.

He moved out the next day, and Mom filed for divorce. A few months later, I received a call from a friend of his who'd been unable to reach Mom. "I spent the weekend here at Roy's place. I'm so sorry to tell you this, but I found him dead in his bed this morning." He'd died of a heart attack in his sleep.

Dying during a divorce, especially one in which the spouse is omitted from the will, particularly complicates the process, and further so when a sizable amount of money and property are involved. Three sons stood to inherit Roy's estate in full but found themselves impeded by laws stating that, as Roy's wife, Mom could not be excluded. If Roy had died before Mom filed for divorce, there were comparatively more cut-and-dried procedures for the division of his property, but the timing of his death created a myriad of complications, even requiring the valuation of each of his assets. "God, if I'd only waited a few months," Mom said to me.

Her life became a mass of hearings, detailed accountings, depositions, and meetings with her lawyer. Then the attorney representing Roy's children died. The proceedings ground to a halt, and it took months to move forward again.

Mom joined me at her dining room table as I waited for a load of laundry to dry. Our washer had bitten the dust, and we couldn't afford to repair or replace it. She tentatively shared that she'd met a musician the night before at a local arts society performance. "So I invited him here to the house afterward, and we talked for hours. He told me, 'I can tell you're a very lonely woman.' He ended up staying the night." She seemed wary of my initial reaction—silence—but my silence came from the shock of hearing her speak openly of her own sexuality.

She left the table, then returned with a publicity shot of him. I took the photo from her and studied his face. Good god, the man still had acne. "How old is this guy?" I asked.

Only seven years older than I am. Oh, Jesus.

For the first time since her twenties, Mom had no husband. Her attorney cautioned her on appearances and warned about dating or giving the impression she'd moved on with her life. When her new boyfriend flew in for a visit, he stayed hidden, closed up in her home for days on end. "He follows me around the house all day like a puppy!" she said.

The first time I met him, he spoke to me of his sexual prowess. "Women always say I'm the best they've ever had in bed."

If I stopped by to see Mom while he visited, she might or might not answer the door. "We peeked out the bedroom shutters and saw you on the porch," she told me one afternoon.

"Why didn't you come to the door?" I'd asked, still too tone deaf to envision her with an active sex life.

So, according to him, he offered great sex. They also had music in common, and he treated her as if she mattered. After years of marital stress and chaos, she seemed to relax somewhat, enjoying the emotional connection and positive attention. But the property settlement battle always loomed, limiting her options in almost every area of her life.

Kyle and I had only accepted enough money from Roy to help us through the first year of school. We became severely strapped for cash, barely keeping our heads above water. Due to our class schedules, both of us had worked only part-time. We mowed lawns on the weekends. I dropped out of school again and took a full-time position with the college of business at the university.

I adored working for Tim—my loud, funny, and irreverent boss. He looked like a stockier version of Larry Hagman, the actor who played J. R. Ewing on *Dallas*, a hugely popular television series at the time. In fact, Tim said he frequently practiced J. R.'s smile in the mirror each morning. Gritted teeth, with one side of his mouth curled up a bit, made him appear rather shark-like at times. Tim employed the smile when discussing anyone who ticked him off. Few risked doing so, for he had star power in the college of business. He hung out in my office so much each day, drinking coffee and smoking cigarettes, I wondered how he got a single thing done. "I'm the dean's fair-haired boy," he said. "I can do no wrong."

His right arm ended at the elbow due to, he said, sticking it in a sausage grinder as a kid. I'd wondered about the veracity of the story, for he struck me as a man who viewed a birth defect as a personal failing. His wife filed for divorce shortly after I started working for him, and with no one at home to fasten the button on the left cuff of his dress shirt, he waited until he got to work every morning, then extended his arm to me for help. We had lunch together every workday and were never at a loss for conversation. He listened to me without judgment, made me laugh, and even attended my ballet performances. He at times introduced me to people as his best friend.

Kyle, a business major, frequently passed by on his way to classes and often wanted to stop in to say hello to me. He'd look through a glass pane on either side of the front door and turn and walk away if he saw Tim seated in my office. "I just don't like that guy," Kyle often said. "There's something weird about him." I chalked it up to jealousy, for when other men showed me attention, it riled him. I traveled often for my job and naturally collected a fair share of business cards with men's names on them.

On more than one occasion, I woke to find he'd gone through my purse and splayed out the men's cards on our kitchen counter as artfully as a casino dealer. He called my hotel room in Houston one evening, raging with jealousy. "You don't love me, and I can't make you! Are you with someone? Who do you have in the room with you? I know you're with someone, Sondra!" He called three times one night, distraught and accusatory.

He had me paged at Pizza Hut as I sat with the other girls from the ballet company, watching a videotape of our recent *Nutcracker* performance. An employee directed me to the phone. "What the hell do you think you're doing?" Kyle yelled. I left the restaurant and came home. We did not discuss his anger. If either one of us knew the true extent of the decay in our marriage, we remained too busy and stressed to address it. Our schedules rarely allowed us to be home at the same time, except for late in the evenings. Sex? Maybe once or twice a year. We worked, went to school, and tried to keep our heads above water financially.

"Kyle gets on my nerves," I confided to Tim as he sat in my office one morning.

He lowered his voice to a whisper. "I can hire someone to kill him if you want." I studied his eyes and noted the J. R. Ewing smile. I lit another cigarette.

After holding the job for over a year, I realized that Mom had never met my wonderful boss, although she'd heard a great deal about him. We stopped by her house after lunch one day, and I introduced her to him. Within a week, they were dating.

Tim prepared my annual performance review, and I scored high in every category. On the evaluation form, he stated his intention that my position be changed to a higher job classification and salary. This required a formal request and evaluation through the red tape of the university, but we foresaw no obstacles. Although thrilled with the promotion, I wondered how Tim couldn't know that Kyle was due to graduate at the end of the semester, and I felt certain he knew the dilemma a promotion created for me. I made no mention of it; I needed time to think.

Numerous companies came to the campus to interview seniors, and Kyle scheduled an interview with a bank in Dallas. He owned only one suit—blue polyester with rather large, widely spaced white pinstripes. A few days prior, I'd taken the only tie that matched to be dry-cleaned. The night before the interview, we went to the dry cleaners and asked them to find the tie and return it to us. Still unprocessed, it remained rather wilted-looking and grimy. I wondered about the impression he might make, but we couldn't afford another suit. He came home one evening a few weeks after the interview and broke into a smile. "Dallas bank," he said.

"Oh, wow," I said. *Oh, shit.* "When do they want an answer?" He mentioned a date, which became a sword hanging over my head demanding a decision. His graduation did not offer me hope as it once had. Knowing we might be free of financial pressure no longer looked like a means to help our marriage. He'd never asked if the job and a move to Dallas outweighed what I'd have to give up. I had a promotion to look forward to. I loved working for Tim and enjoyed my coworkers. I loved dancing in the ballet company. I hadn't let Kyle know of my seesawing emotions or that my resolve waffled by the hour.

I had, however, confided my uncertainty to Mom. "Well, either you love Kyle enough to go with him or you don't," she said. I knew I still loved him. I didn't know if I still liked him.

A few nights later he came through the door and found me at the dining room table in the kitchen. I looked up at his beaming smile. "Twenty-one thousand five hundred a year," he said. "I accepted the job this morning."

I'd often noted how stupid most people looked with their

mouths hanging open. I shut mine. He waited for a sign of happiness. A sign that maybe I was proud of him. A hint of gratitude for the bright future the job might offer us. But there hadn't been an *us* since we married. "I'm not going," I said.

His smile wavered as he waited, as if I were only milliseconds away from breaking out into laughter over a practical joke I'd chosen to play on him. But earlier that day, Tim and I had looked at an efficiency apartment for me to rent. I'd put down a deposit—Tim wrote the check—for if I had not, I knew for certain I'd lose my nerve. "What do you mean, you're not going?" Kyle said.

"I'm not going with you."

His expression transitioned through varying shades of confusion, then turned stony. "Fine. Do what you want," he said. He turned and went to the bedroom to change clothes.

We avoided eye contact as we moved wordlessly around and past one another whenever our schedules intersected at the house. Shortly after we'd married, he'd learned that his anger easily cowed me, and he'd adopted the silent treatment as his weapon of choice when I failed to see things his way. But after days of silence and seeing no capitulation, nor my usual servile attempts to break the ice, he folded. "I called around today, trying to find counseling for us. I mean, it has to be ministers because of the cost. But can we at least talk to someone? Then, if you still don't want to go . . ."

I agreed, but only because I secretly hoped to have a professional make the decision for me, to declare our marriage hopelessly dysfunctional—flat-out dead—then advise that we cut our losses, part as friends, and go our merry ways. I heard nothing more about counseling until the following weekend. As I lay sunbathing in the backyard, I heard a knock at the front door, then the sound of Kyle talking to someone. "Sondra, can you get in here?" he called out. Not knowing he'd invited someone into our home, I came inside dressed in a tiny bikini. The man introduced himself as the pastor of a local Baptist church.

"Kyle contacted me last week about getting some help," he said. Instead of excusing myself to change clothes, I sat down on the couch. Kyle joined me. The pastor took a seat in the rocking chair by the front door and addressed me directly. "The way I see it, the issue is that Kyle accepted a job offer without discussing it with you. He did so without considering the numerous changes and adjustments you'd have to make."

Bingo.

He shifted his focus to Kyle. "Kyle, she's your wife. You have to include her in your decisions."

"Oh, wow. I guess you're right," Kyle said. He said it far too quickly for me to believe he'd had anything remotely resembling an epiphany.

The pastor left our house after only a few minutes. I went back outside to work on my tan. *Okay, so we talked to someone. Done.*

But a Christian therapist returned Kyle's call the following week with the offer of charging us on a sliding scale. "He promised he won't preach to us," Kyle assured me, "so I booked an appointment." After sitting down in front of the man, Kyle mentioned the Dallas conundrum, and I mentioned our dead sex life. I again secretly hoped for the performance of last rites on the marriage. No such luck.

"It's all about what I call the Three C's," the therapist announced. He held a large poster board on his lap and, although we were only about six feet away from him, used a pointer on each section of his obviously homemade visual. "Caring, Chemistry, and Communication. I can't do much about the caring part, and I can't do a single thing about chemistry. But let's work on communication."

We had to listen to tapes of couples struggling to share their feelings. I wanted to slap the actress, who feigned tear-filled vulnerability while communicating with her actor-husband. "I (sniff) just . . . just . . . feel so . . . (sniff) . . . small when you . . ."

Jesus H. Christ, lady. Just spit it out.

We practiced focused listening, some sort of parroting technique. One of us made a statement, then the other repeated it word for word. "We never talk. You don't even pay attention to me," I said.

"So, what I hear you saying is that we never talk, and I don't even pay attention to you," Kyle said.

"I don't feel like I matter," I said.

"What I hear you saying is that you don't feel like you matter," Kyle said.

We listened to the mealy-mouthed actors and repeated each other's statements for almost an hour. The therapist assigned reading from a book called *The Gift of Sex*. "God created sex not only for procreation but for human enjoyment," he informed us. "It's his special gift to married couples."

Gift, my ass.

A couple of weeks later, I came into work and picked up on an odd tension. The second-in-command in our department, an unfailingly cheerful woman, frowned at me as she went into her office. I put my purse down on my desk and went to the storage room for coffee. I couldn't recall a time when Tim arrived at the office before I did, but he stood in front of the coffee maker, already pouring a cup. He looked as if he hadn't slept all night. "You look terrible," I said.

"I feel like hammered shit," he said. He came into my office as he did every morning, sat down in his usual chair, then fired me. "You think your way of doing things is always the best way. I just can't have someone like you working for me. And you've been spreading your personal problems all over the college of business."

I'd told an acquaintance down the hall in Administration that I felt torn about moving, but had discussed the issue with no one else but Tim. *"Never let a man know he's hurt you."* I nodded, then packed up my desk. I walked out, got in my car, and headed for home. As I neared my street, I slowed, then turned toward Mom's house instead. I knocked on her front door and opened it a crack. "Mom?" I called out. "It's me."

"In here," she said.

I found her in her robe in the kitchen, working at the sink. As I poured out the story of my firing, I spoke to her profile. She didn't make eye contact or stop washing dishes and remained expressionless as I voiced my shock and confusion. "Well, I know a lot more about this situation than you think," she finally said.

"What do you mean?"

She continued to work silently with something on the counter.

"Mom, what? What do you know?"

She still had not looked at me. A sickening rush of reality hit as I watched her expressionless face. She and Tim were still dating, and he'd no doubt already provided his side of the story. She'd known in advance that he planned to fire me that morning and obviously believed I deserved it. I rued the day I'd introduced them to one another. I picked up my purse and went home.

Kyle went with me to the university the next day to talk to Larry, the assistant dean, with whom I'd had a good working relationship. Kyle asked if I could count on a good reference from him when I started applying for jobs. Larry kept his eyes cast downward, shuffled papers back and forth on his desk, and did not look at me. "You can have them call for a reference, but I'll tell them exactly what Tim told me." I did not ask what that was.

The burning humiliation and anger drove me to envision retaliation against Tim, to do anything that might cause him pain or embarrassment. The depth of my need to exact brutal revenge scared me. But, as "the dean's fair-haired boy," Tim's actions wouldn't even warrant a wrist slap by the university. I knew of no way to even the score.

I no longer had a job, the boss I adored had betrayed me, and Mom had taken his side against me. Dallas, here we come.

Several people from the bank where Kyle worked often met at Studebaker's, a 1950s-style nightclub, during rush hour. Most lived on the far outskirts of Dallas, and waiting out the traffic proved to be more fun at a bar than on the freeway. I met Kyle and his coworkers at the bar from time to time for drinks. One evening I turned away from a conversation and saw Tim the moment he turned and saw me. He stood at the bar with a man I didn't recognize, probably a fellow professor or financial professional, as Tim traveled from time to time for speaking engagements or to lead continuing professional education seminars. I walked over and hugged him. He hugged me back. "I never did anything to hurt you," I said, and started to cry.

"I know," he said.

I turned away and returned to our group, people who proved to be a particularly protective lot when looking out for their own. Kyle's demeanor upon seeing Tim got their hackles up, especially when they saw my tears. Tim had about ten sets of hostile eyes on him. He quickly said something to the man with him, and they left the bar. "Why are you crying?" one of the women asked me.

"I used to work for him," I said.

"So, you worked for him. It's not like you were in love with him or anything, right?"

"I think I once was," I said.

Chapter Fourteen

Earning more money did reduce the stress between us, but our time in Dallas created the sensation of treading water. Kyle watched television every night and rooted for the Cowboys every weekend. We worked all week, then spent hours playing water volleyball at the apartment complex pool every Saturday. I continued to attend his softball games. I took a few courses toward my degree at UT-Dallas. We gave up trying to fix our sex life. We no longer bothered to discuss it. So much for the Three C's.

After a year or so, the Czech ballet master from the civic ballet invited me back for a guest appearance. Of course, I stayed with Mom, and we shared the master bedroom, leaving the guest room for my grandmother, who planned to fly in the day of the performance. I did not ask Mom if she and Tim still dated, nor did she volunteer the information. We did not discuss him at all.

One of Mom's new boyfriends—Mike—appeared at the house every night at dinnertime and remained until around two in the morning. I could not for the life of me figure out what they did every night while I tried to sleep, but they seemed constantly in motion, and one night I could swear I heard them moving furniture. They often forgot to adjust the volume of the stereo when they turned it on, and Julio Iglesias's voice jarred me alert as I struggled for hours to relax enough to fall asleep.

Mom agreed to dinner plans one evening with a doctor friend of hers, and we waited for his call to tell us when to meet him. When eight o'clock came and went with no word, I begged off to try to get some sleep. The phone rang around one in the morning, and Mom came into the master bedroom to answer it. It took a few minutes for her to make the doctor understand why dinner after midnight was out of the question. He'd sounded drunk or medicated, she told me the next morning, and had lost all sense of time. And I'd lost yet another night of sleep.

By the time performance night arrived, I'd added severe sleep-deprivation to my list of physical woes. My dancing suffered—my knotted leg muscles couldn't respond to the demands, and I felt weak, wobbly, and entirely exhausted. I knew I'd embarrassed myself by my performance. But the week mercifully ended, and I had an early flight back to Dallas the next morning. A woman associated with the ballet company threw a party for the dancers, and the ballet master and I sat on the floor by one another, petted the lady's dog as we talked, and drank wine for hours. After about five glasses, I leaned over and kissed him on the mouth.

We'd always had heat between us but had never acted on it. The combination of muscle and grace in a man rarely failed to move me into a state of lust. I loved how he pronounced certain English words. "Relax your elbah," he'd say when adjusting my arm position. Mostly, his eyes got to me—so dark, almost black. Mysterious and intense.

His wife had been pregnant for part of the time I'd known him. He frequently lost his temper and belittled her when I saw them together. She did not attend the party that night and may or may not have attended the performance due to having a young child at home. She never showed warmth toward me, surely noting the palpable chemistry I shared with her husband, but he and I had, so far, behaved.

He agreed to drop me off at Mom's house. On the way, he pulled off the road and parked by a small pond. We crawled into the back seat of his car. He moved on top of me and fumbled under my dress. The cramped space didn't allow for easy removal of my pantyhose and underwear, but we somehow managed. Given the ineffectual prodding going on as he lay on top of me, I couldn't tell if what poked and poked at me qualified as an erection, as the lack of space greatly restricted our movements. "I cannot do," he finally said. Alas, a sad debut for the balletomane, who admitted to being too drunk to perform. I was too drunk to care. We lay there a while, chatting about nothing I can recall, then got dressed and climbed back into the front seat. "I fail as man," he said, starting the car.

Mom had locked the front door of her house, and my knocking woke her. When she let me in, I silently moved past her and went to bed. Drunk and past exhaustion, I slept. The next morning, I rolled over and looked at the clock on the bedside table. My flight left in an hour, but no one had thought to wake me. Unshowered, with the previous night's stage makeup smeared across my face, nauseatingly hungover and riddled with guilt, I made the flight. I stared out the window of the plane, wondering how long it took for a sexually transmitted disease to make itself known. *Did he enter me far enough to give me an STD? Could he transmit something just by rubbing against me?* The cold light of day had me scared so straight, I vowed never, never, ever to even *think* of screwing around on Kyle again. I felt certain that when he picked me up at the airport, he'd sense my guilt as soon as the plane met the tarmac.

"Hey, what do you think about my transferring to Seattle?" he asked as we drove home. Glare hit my eyes through the windshield, and I fought back the urge to vomit. I looked at him and shrugged. I loved that this new development might divert his attention from me even more than usual, for my gnawing guilt threatened to eat a hole through my stomach. Back at the apartment that afternoon, still hungover and insane with exhaustion, I lay stretched out on the couch and listened to him talk about the job offer. I thought I might drop off to sleep as the details dribbled out, but then he tugged at my ankle. "Sondra, what the hell happened there?"

My eyes shot open. I jerked my foot away, but he took hold of the other and leaned in toward it. "My god, your feet!" Both feet had blisters, some oozing and even bloody, from pointe shoes and five long days of rehearsal. "You should see yourself!" he said. "You look like you haven't slept in a month. You look like a zombie! What the hell happened there?"

"Nothing!" I said. "Nothing happened there." I tried to pull away, but he held tight.

"Do you not even get how much your mother abuses you?"

"She doesn't abuse me; I just didn't get any sleep! She has another boyfriend, they were up late, people called at all hours—"

"You don't think she could have made some accommodation for you? She treats you like an afterthought!"

I started to cry, jerked my foot out of his grasp, and ran into the bedroom. "She doesn't abuse me!" I called out as I swung the door shut behind me.

A few months later, Mom called. By then I rarely knew how to get in touch with her. She said she and the musician, who lived in New York, were still a couple and she traveled often to see him. She also mentioned a new man she referred to as the Colonel. "We've been crawlin' through the heathers of Scotland in search of wild boar," she said. "I'm drivin' through Dallas tomorrow and want to stop off and visit you."

She arrived late the next evening. Dinnertime had long passed, so I went ahead and made up the couch for her. "We'll see you in the morning and make a nice breakfast for you," I said. When we got up around six, we found her sheets and blanket neatly folded on the couch. She was long gone. I thought of the stealth she'd had to employ to escape our apartment. I hadn't even heard the toilet flush, although the bathroom was only three steps from our bedroom. I pictured her leaving before dawn, suitcase in hand, and slowly, slowly, slowly pulling our front door shut to avoid making the slightest click.

"I swear, Sondra. One day you're going to be standing out on the interstate holding up a 'HI, MOM' sign when she drives by," Kyle said.

She called in August to wish me a happy birthday. We hadn't spoken in several weeks. "And just because we don't talk much, it doesn't mean I don't love you," she said.

"Okay," I said. When I hung up, Kyle asked why she'd called. "To wish me a happy birthday," I said.

"But it's not your birthday."

"Yes, it is."

"Your birthday isn't until next week."

"My birthday is today."

"No, it isn't."

"Yes, it is."

"Sondra, today is not your birthday," he said, as if speaking to a toddler. But later that day, he brought home a pink stuffed pig with three little piglets hanging off the side. I'd gasped and pointed and gone teary-eyed over the pig after seeing it given to a hospital patient on *St. Elsewhere*, one of our favorite television shows. "Happy birthday," Kyle said, handing it to me.

Chapter Fifteen

Kyle's job transfer came through, and we arrived in Seattle in the summer of '84. I got a job as a secretary at a small foreign bank downtown after practice typing for two days to qualify for the 45 WPM requirement for the position. We still had only one car, so I lived by Kyle's work schedule. He insisted on being at his desk by seven thirty, and he rarely left until after six. He claimed dropping me off at work in the mornings risked making him late. He'd cruise down the steep hill that led to his bank, always calibrating his speed to coincide with the change of the upcoming traffic light. My instructions were to jump out quickly before he made the final turn in front of his building. "Go, go, go!" he'd yell. "I'm gonna miss the light!" It riled him to have to bring the car to a complete stop.

I'd jump out of the car and backtrack several blocks to my job. I kept my dress shoes, purse, and a book in a shoulder bag. After work, I'd put my tennis shoes back on and trudge through downtown to his bank, sometimes waiting for hours until he finished his work. He never allowed me to take the wheel and took it upon himself to decide whether we needed to stop off at the dry cleaners or grocery store. He still kept the checkbook and took control over which foods we'd buy. "Is it okay if we get this?" I'd ask, holding out a product for him to inspect. If he decided we might have wine with dinner, he chose it.

I'd moved closer to obtaining my degree after taking courses in Dallas, but Kyle no longer saw a need for me to pursue further education. "I have a degree now, so you don't need one," he said. "Well, I think I might want an MBA one day," I said. "It sounds kinda cool."

"Your math skills are too weak to ever get a business degree, Sondra." I believed him.

Mom continued to ask when I planned to finish school, and I continued to defend Kyle's reasoning. If we couldn't afford a second car, we surely couldn't afford my tuition. And the transportation logistics! The limitations this placed on me were insanely restrictive. I settled for a nighttime accounting course offered a few streets over from Kyle's bank. "I have to buy a calculator," I told him. "It costs ten dollars. Is that okay?" He gave his permission for the expense. I aced the course, signed up for a second, and then a third.

I'd landed a new job and started working for a brilliant man. He'd played sports in college and had a particularly solid, stocky physique. Wide, muscular shoulders and a confident swagger were offset with dark brown, expressive eyes. He'd get me laughing so hard, I thought I might fall out of my chair, pee in my pants, or both. His wife was about eight months pregnant when I started working for him, and he casually mentioned that he refused to have sex with her once she started to show, finding the idea a turn-off. She got pregnant with their second child several months after delivering the first, and he mentioned that they'd again stopped having sex.

He and I had lunch together almost every day. One afternoon at Jack in the Box—our favorite downtown haunt—he shared how he dealt with his young son's crying. "I press him really close to my chest and hold him so tight he can barely move."

"I wish you'd do that to me," I said.

He studied my face for a moment, looked down at the table, looked out the window, then back at me. "I don't even know what to say," he said.

Two days later, we sneaked away at lunchtime and had unprotected sex in my unmade marital waterbed. He seemed to enjoy it well enough, but fear of being caught prevented me from relaxing and fully responding. And my Chihuahua, which I'd neglected to toss out of the bedroom before we started, barked the entire time. Rumpled looking and stressed, I returned to the office. A few weeks later, a company reorganization transferred me to a different department, and the seven floors that separated us severely limited my ability to see or talk to him. For weeks on end, it felt as if every thought revolved around devising a way to catch sight of him, have lunch with him, or even chat for a few minutes. At home I feigned business as usual while trying to hide my growing obsession. He'd flipped a switch in me that I could not turn off, so desperate was my need for sexual intimacy and physical touch. My body burned for him. My nipples grew hard at the memory of his mouth on them. My underwear turned warm and wet at the thought of having him inside me again.

I had no appetite, and pounds fell off me. I lost all ability to concentrate on my work. Our company went through a huge upheaval, and most employees had to find jobs elsewhere, my ex-boss included. Although only one block away, the new company where he worked may as well have been on the moon. He didn't need a lovesick mistress placing demands on his limited time, and I called him only once, under the guise of asking about a Lotus 1-2-3 macro he'd once taught me. I spent the rest of my time waiting for him to throw me some sort of bone and could barely contain my joy when he finally called and asked me to lunch the following week.

He called about thirty minutes before our lunch date. "I've been doing some thinking," he said.

"Okay," I said, hopefully.

"Well, I'm going to be a father again in a few months . . ."

"Uh-huh."

"You know . . . my conscience . . . ," he said. "I feel too guilty doing this."

"Oh."

"You know . . . so, I have to break this off. I just can't—"

I squeezed the phone receiver so hard I thought it might crack open. "I understand. I really do."

"Sorry," he said.

"Okay. Thanks," I said, my eyes filling with tears.

When he hung up, I put my hand over my mouth to stifle my wail.

Chapter Sixteen

Dad surprised me by calling me at work one afternoon, as most of our conversations took place on the weekends. "I called to tell you I'm divorced," he said.

"You mean you're getting a divorce?"

"No. I'm already divorced."

"What in the world—"

"Patsy kept saying God wanted her to leave me. I took her to Mexico, and we patched things up. When we got back, she started up with the 'God wants me to leave you' bit. So I took her to Mexico again," he said.

"And?"

"And I thought we patched things up."

"I don't understand," I said.

"Sure enough, the God stuff started again. Just in case, I'd left all the filings and paperwork active. I couldn't afford another trip to Mexico."

The phone rang in the dark on a Saturday morning. I fumbled around for the receiver and croaked a hello.

"Hi! I wanted you and my boyfriend to talk. We've decided to get married."

I looked over Kyle's body at the clock on the bedside table and moaned. "Mom. It's five in the morning."

"I just never can get these time differences straight!" she said, laughing. "Say hi to him."

"Mom, really—"

"Here. Talk to him," she said excitedly, handing the phone over.

After a few heys and how-is-it-goings, the conversation ended. "Don't fuck this up," I mumbled, hanging up the phone. A few days later, Mom and I talked again. It had only been a few months since her years-long battle over Roy's estate ended, and I didn't see how she could be anything but bruised and wartorn after such a protracted fight. "Why are you getting married again?" I asked.

"I'm just so tired of being alone," she said. It didn't seem to me that she'd been alone at all.

A few months later, she and her boyfriend came to town to attend a convention related to his work. I met them at their hotel, where the three of us planned to have dinner. But before we'd even ordered, a business associate invited himself to sit with us and didn't stop talking for an hour and a half. Mom and I barely spoke to one another; I suppose we considered it rude to speak over the man's droning. Before leaving for home, I mentioned that I worked walking distance from the hotel and could easily come over the next day to have lunch with her. "I can't," she said. "I accidentally left all of my jewelry at home, and I'll need to buy more to wear to the evening events."

"But I can come over and go with you," I said.

"No, I really can't. I don't have time for lunch."

"But, Mom, I'm just two blocks away."

"I don't have time," she said.

When we spoke on the phone the next day, I asked how her shopping went. "Oh, I found all my jewelry in my suitcase. I didn't have to buy more after all," she said.

"Well, are you going to be able to come out and see our place?"

"No, we won't have time. They keep us busy every night with these dinners and all." But I learned later that she and her boyfriend had rented a limo for the evening and had ridden down to Carlsbad to see one of his relatives. "We spent four hours in the car just to get there and back," she said, sighing.

"So *now* can you come to our house?" I asked.

"No. We're leaving tomorrow, and I have to pack. But why don't you and Kyle come downtown tonight and have dinner with us?"

So, Kyle and I got home from work, changed our clothes, then drove back downtown. This time, her boyfriend's brother and his wife joined us, and they made no effort to participate in conversation. Anything said to the wife was met with a mono-syllabic response. The mood was tense and very little was said.

"That's Julie Andrews at the next table," Mom said. By god, it was. I remember little else from that evening, except that no one seemed the least bit interested in Kyle's and my presence, not even Mom. When she left town the next day, it was a relief.

Chapter Seventeen

Kyle determined that since he made more money, he could spend more. My expendable income would be less, he said, based on my lower salary. He budgeted $100 a month to cover my lunches during the week, nail appointments, clothes, and various incidentals. I didn't respond, but I'd reached the point where I'd try anything to placate him.

Taking the time to pay bills proved inconvenient for him, so I took over the responsibility, then turned the checkbook back over to him. I sat in the kitchen one evening writing checks and remembered to mention that I'd paid a few medical co-pays and parking expenses for doctor appointments that month. "I don't have to pay for medical out of my one hundred, do I?"

He stopped on his way past the kitchen table. "Do you have receipts?" he asked.

I stopped writing a check, looked up, and finally saw him. The air of superiority. The pathetic need to control more and more of my being. The belief that my upkeep should cost him as little as possible. I wanted to slap that supercilious bearing right the fuck off his face. I rose from my chair so forcefully, it rolled back and slammed into the wall. "I'm fucking out of here!" I yelled.

"So, what brings you here?" Roxanne, my new therapist, asked.

"My husband and I don't have sex," I said.

Her mouth dropped open. "You don't have sex?"

"No. Hardly ever. And he's always finding fault with me. It's like nothing I ever do is right. I don't even want to stay married to him. But I can't think. I can't plan."

"Well, what does he do that bothers you?" Roxanne asked, her pen poised over the legal pad on her lap.

"He leaves the refrigerator door open."

Her eyes widened. "He leaves the refrigerator door open?"

I took her surprised expression to mean that she, too, viewed this as a truly egregious offense. When put on the spot, I could think of no other faults of his, for I'd come to view him as the more mature and worldly one, the person naturally in charge, and myself as the feeble-minded half of the marriage that needed to be led along—and worse, tolerated—due to my incompetence, of which he frequently reminded me and anyone else who would listen.

"Sondra thinks ATMs are an endless source of money," he told a circle of his banking coworkers over dinner. And because I once reached for a knife on the counter by the stove and stirred a pot with it, he thought it funny to relate yet another one of my idiotic quirks. "She stirs things with knives." People laughed at his stories, and I'd try to crack a smile. I'd begun to wonder what it said about him, really, that he chose to marry a woman so ditzy, a woman with so few redeeming qualities. "But she's a good kid when she's asleep," he'd add.

Roxanne asked me to write down three requirements that had to be met for me to stay in the marriage. "I'm not telling you to stay," she said. "But I can help you make a decision." That evening, with a shaking voice, I told Kyle I'd seen a therapist that morning. His eyes narrowed and his face hardened. I handed over the list.

1. We will see a therapist.
2. I will have my own car and money.
3. I will go back to school.

He read it, wadded it in a ball, and threw it in my face. "This is bullshit!" he said.

I went upstairs and worked on my plan to exit the marriage. The next day, I called universities and inquired about registration for the upcoming semester. I enrolled and chose a major in business administration. When Kyle saw the growing to-do list and scribbled notes spread out on our bed, my intentions and determination were made crystal clear. After days of giving me the silent treatment, he finally spoke. "I'll go see the therapist with you," he said.

After Roxanne ushered us into her office, Kyle moved to the far end of the couch, away from me, adjusted a pillow in the corner, and sat facing us at an angle. "Sorry for how this looks," he said, "but it's easier on my back."

"It's okay, Kyle. Thanks for coming. I'm Roxanne."

He leaned forward and started singing the song by the Police, even adding a bit of a rasping quality to his voice as Sting did when drawing out the name. "Roxanne. You don't have to put on the red light. Roooooooooxanne."

"You know," she said, "that's the one reason I hate that my mother ever named me Roxanne." Kyle eased back into his corner of the couch, and she cut to the chase. "Okay. For the next few weeks, you two are not allowed to have sex. Don't even think about having sex. It's off the table. Okay?" Roxanne said. "Kyle, is there anything Sondra does during sex that you don't like?"

"No, I like everything she does."

"Sondra? What do you think about sex with Kyle?"

"It all feels so mechanical to me," I said.

Roxanne met with Kyle alone the next time. Then I came in to talk to her by myself. "You should have seen his expression when you said sex with him feels mechanical. It seemed to crush him."

When Kyle and I returned for a joint session, Roxanne asked him what he wanted from the marriage. His eyes filled with tears. "All I want is a peaceful, normal life."

I then agreed to postpone any plans for divorce, at least long enough to give therapy a chance at saving the marriage. I did not confess that I stayed only because I saw no way to afford school without his income. I'd left three schools due to his job transfers, and I refused to allow anything to stop me this time from getting my degree.

I'd invested seven years in the marriage. I could endure another year and a half.

Not only did I start night classes, I accepted a position as accounting manager for a major real estate company. I'd taken three accounting classes, but this hardly made me an expert. As soon as I accepted the position, I foresaw embarrassment and failure. The feeling so overwhelmed me, I began pacing back and forth in the kitchen, eyeing the phone, wanting to call someone, anyone, who might help make the fear go away. Then I heard a voice, as if an actual something or someone hovered over my head speaking to me. "You know what you need?" it gently whispered.

The entity felt so real, so present. I looked at the ceiling. "What?" I asked it.

"Alcohol," it said.

Fine by me. I went to the liquor store down the street and bought a bottle of white wine. Up to that point in my marriage, I had never bought alcohol on my own—Kyle controlled whether we drank at home. He might buy wine a few times a month to share over dinner, but the two of us never finished an entire bottle in one sitting. Unfinished wine eventually grew bitter and sour in the fridge, and I'd pour it down the drain. But that evening, I popped open *my* bottle and dove into the icy and tart liquid. In less than an hour, I'd drunk enough confidence to call a guy from my study group at school to chat, ramble, and gush about my excitement over the new job.

Wine—my gentle, soothing, and supportive new best friend—became everything I needed her to be. I no longer felt lonely and soon found I could handle just about anything as long as she awaited me every night at home. I felt almost . . . happy. She welcomed me—comforted me, even—from where she stood on the bottom shelf of the refrigerator door. It became her special place, and I frequently checked the remaining amount of nurturing she had left to offer. When I could polish off most of a bottle by myself, I made sure I stopped off at the liquor store every night on my way home, bought the same brand, then drank the new bottle down to the level of the previous one, believing I could fool Kyle into thinking I drank far less than I did.

It's highly unlikely I fooled him, but he didn't dare rock the boat. I hadn't filed for divorce, I came home every night, and the presence of my warm and breathing body in the house provided him with the illusion of normalcy. He'd agreed to my demands: I had free access to the checkbook, I attended college, I had my own car, and he and I had met with Roxanne several times, although I'd quickly allowed therapy to be crowded out by my new job and night classes. Some days I left for work before seven in the morning and didn't get home from school until ten at night. I excelled in the job and took on the management of an accounting system conversion for our branch of the company. The days proved challenging and seemingly endless, and I fed on not only the stress of it all but the priceless sense of empowerment that came from knowing I'd be able to support myself financially.

The night I completed my last class requirement for a bachelor of business administration, I cried with joy all the way home. On the morning of graduation ceremonies, Kyle came to me with a sheepish look. "You don't mind if I play golf instead of going, do you?" he asked.

Nope. Not a bit. I'd made two wonderful friends at school and hoped to spend the rest of the afternoon with them, celebrating. But it turned out, they had coworkers and family in attendance, and I didn't feel right intruding. I went home and left messages for them, to see if maybe we could get together later that evening, but didn't hear back.

I hadn't felt so lonely in years. I opened the refrigerator, brought my best friend to the table, sat down, and celebrated.

In the car, on our way to a party with his coworkers, Kyle gave me instructions on how to behave. "Why are you telling me how to act?" I asked.

"I just want people to like you," he said.

My wine friend gave me a voice—a rather strident one. I assumed people preferred the louder, more brazen me over the reserved and excruciatingly self-conscious version they'd previously known. I know I did. Since marrying Kyle, my spark had dimmed severely. I'd felt my diminishment. Alcohol provided a take-me-or-leave-me bravery, and additional friendships had developed with the new and improved version of me.

At the party that night, Thomas and I stood drunkenly in the host's kitchen and poured several different kinds of liquor into a blender. We added ice, mixed it all together, and drank a few large gulps. He shrugged and added more alcohol. We stumbled, giggling, out to the far part of the backyard among dark shadows of trees. Amid the sounds of music, loud conversations, and laughter, I stepped in close and kissed him, unzipped his pants, then bent over and took him into my mouth. "Oh, Sondra," he moaned as he came.

I had just blown Kyle's best friend. I didn't care that he didn't reciprocate in any way; I'd provided sex to a man I liked, and at least experienced what felt like intimacy through the pleasure I'd given him. Such was the courage I'd gotten from a bottle that night. I paid for it the next day with shame and an excruciating hangover. But by three in the afternoon, I felt well enough to drink again. I warned myself to simply behave better in the future and preferred to concentrate on what I viewed as the numerous benefits of alcohol.

While sitting at the kitchen table paying bills one evening, I took out pen and paper and wrote to Vance, with whom I'd had no contact in almost fifteen years. Three glasses of wine made the words come easily. I started with an apology for my hateful treatment of him, then briefly mentioned my several-year-long marriage, Greyson's marriage, and my return to school. I closed with the assurance that my behavior toward him had been nothing personal and that any man who came through the door at that time of my life would have met the same hostility. Whether or not these statements were true I did not know, but it seemed he had tried his hardest to find a bridge of reconciliation with me during the three years he'd been married to Mom, only to be met with my hostility and rejection at every turn. I mailed the letter to his medical practice in Houston, the address for which I still remembered. In less than a week, I received a reply.

Dear Cissie:

What a wonderful and moving surprise to hear from you! You should know my reaction to your letter. My heart came up in my throat and tears came to my eyes. I certainly haven't been angry for the problems we had. That holds true for Greyson also who was in a terrible spot and was confronted with a new father figure at an important point in his life. I am very happy for each of you and for your happy marriages.

Please think no more of forgiveness except to forgive me for the ways in which I was impatient with you. We both

apparently did enough things right that we each have warm
feelings toward the other.
   I love you
   Vance

His ability to forgive so graciously stunned me. I felt struck
as well by many of his assumptions. I'd said nothing about a
happy marriage, mine or Greyson's; in fact, Greyson and his
wife divorced shortly thereafter. But I'd come to find that people
assumed a marriage must be happy if the two parties remained
in it.

I did not have a happy marriage, but I remained. Most of my
perceived needs were sufficiently met by wine. No matter how
my day went, the night promised comfort when spent with a bottle. Kyle had become obsessed with golf by this time and spent
every evening at a small pitch and putt nearby. I had the additional security of his income but rarely had to interact with him.
The status quo felt doable. After all, it wasn't as if he hit me, ran
around on me, or called me names.

Chapter Eighteen

My ex-boss called and asked me to lunch, saying he only wanted to talk. I waited at the top of a long set of stairs in front of a downtown cafeteria and watched him approach from the end of the block. His athleticism made his stride graceful and slightly cocky at the same time, and the broad shoulders and large biceps that used to enfold me made him identifiable even from far down the street. When he stood in front of me at the top of the stairs, he reached out for a hug. I flinched and backed away. "It's okay," he said. "It's okay to do this." My body went stiff in his arms.

While we ate, I had trouble hearing him over the shattering glasses a waitress dropped, busboys slamming dishes into bins, silverware clinking on plates, and the weird hum a hundred or so voices make. I watched his gorgeous mouth while he stated his case. "I don't see why we can't be friends," he said.

He was back in the saddle—my grateful saddle—within forty-eight hours. Then he broke it off again. A few weeks later, he called and asked me to come see him after work. He recommended we sit in his car in the parking garage, as we'd have no privacy in his office. Our conversation quickly turned nonverbal. Afterward, I pulled out my compact mirror and set about repairing my makeup.

"Guess what? My wife's gonna have another baby."

"Huh?" I said dully, applying my lipstick.

"Just found out. I'm going to be a father again. Isn't it great?"

"Why the hell did you go and do that?" I yelled, snapping my compact shut.

"I really like kids," he said.

Really? That's a defense? That's a reason? That piece-of-crap response? Why, yes. The perfect response for a pathetic sort of woman, one who'd always returned to you whenever summoned. The kind who, not five minutes ago, gave you a blow job in your car, in a dark and dirty downtown parking garage. The kind you could fuck on the side while trying to get your wife pregnant. Then, when your wife started to show, when her expanding stomach grew unattractive to you, the same pathetic woman surely still waited for you, all hot and eager to please. And just in case you need a reminder: dump this rather pathetic woman as soon as your wife delivers the baby.

I'd always hoped that he regarded me as no common, everyday mistress. Had I not fulfilled my role far beyond the call of duty? I hadn't made a pest of myself. I'd never threatened to tell his wife. I'd asked for no gifts, no nice dinners, no hotel room in which to offer myself. I thought of the number of times he'd asked me to lunch, dismissed me, lured me back in, had sex with me, broken up, then called soon after, only to have me willingly run to him all over again. Throughout, I'd held on to a small shard of hope that he'd leave his wife for me. If they only had one child? Maybe. Two? Not so fast. Three? *Not on your life, you weak, needy, gullible, amoral, desperate, naive, doormat, idiot slut-lump of mistress flesh.*

But the man never lied to me. The realization so surely and thoroughly seeped into my brain: we'd have no future together, and he'd never once promised one. Just because every fiber of my being cried out for what he gave me, it didn't mean he felt the same. When he accepted a job transfer out of state, his departure didn't feel like an exit from my life but an excision. No goodbye hug, no talk of memories over a cup of coffee, no Final Farewell Fuck.

Kyle asked about him when he took me out to dinner for my birthday at a nearby restaurant. "He moved away a few months ago," I said.

"Thank god that affair's over."

I couldn't look up from my plate. "So, you suspected an affair but said nothing about it?" I took a stab at a small how-ludicrous-to-suspect-me-of-adultery smile.

"I knew you'd be back when you were ready," he said. I concentrated on my dinner and tried not to look sheepish. He talked at me about FCC regulation issues related to his job.

My ex-boss came to town a few months later. We ended up in bed, but only because I'd turned the tables on him and had sex purely for *my* satisfaction. "You know," he said as I lay in his arms. "There will never come a time in my life when I won't think about you and wonder how you are." He said he'd be back soon and promised to call. He never did. I no longer cared.

Chapter Nineteen

A feeling came over me at work that I needed to see my father, and I scheduled a trip to Houston to visit him. The night before my flight, his new wife of two years called to tell me she'd taken him to the emergency room for searing chest pain. The doctors attempted a balloon angioplasty, found his arteries too clogged for the procedure, and scheduled an emergency bypass. I arrived at the hospital while he was in surgery but was allowed to see him later that afternoon. The respirator kept him flat on his back. When he heard my voice, he reached out. I stepped in closer, and he caressed my face. "That's right, honey. That's your sweet Sondra," his wife said.

Three days after surgery, his doctors struggled unsuccessfully to regulate his heartbeat with his oxygen intake. Dad died of respiratory distress.

When I came home, there were no condolences from Kyle. Instead, I found he'd wired the kitchen sink trap to the drain during my absence. He'd scolded me many a time for not returning it to its proper place after emptying food scraps from it. I'd put our sink at great risk of clogging, he'd frequently warned me. I unwired the trap, then sat down at the table to pay bills. A large glass of wine never left my side that evening. "You're drinking a lot tonight," Kyle said.

"Yep. I sure am."

He'd leave me alone for a while, then return to stand by the table and observe me. "You really are drinking a lot. That's a lot of wine."

"Yeah, it is. My father died. Remember?"

He returned a while later to stare at me a bit more, but I didn't look up. Soon, I went to bed.

When I started my car the next morning, I found that while I'd been away, he'd changed all my radio station settings to his favorites. As I tried to reset them, he stepped out of the house and came over to my car. I rolled down the window and waited for him to say something. Instead, he silently stared at me. I sighed and stared back. "You really drank a lot last night," he said.

"You wanna screw?" I asked. He looked confused, then raised an eyebrow and nodded. I handed him a screw I'd found minutes before on the garage floor. He turned and went in the house. I backed out of the garage and headed to the airport. I was due in North Carolina for Mom's fifth wedding.

Joan, one of Mom's friends from the time she'd been married to Roy, approached me at the reception. I recognized her immediately and tried to keep my eyes up and away from the boob job she'd gotten since I last saw her. She pulled me in for a hug, which felt as if I'd been pressed against two basketballs, dangerously overfilled with air. She somehow remembered a great deal about me. "You used to work for Tim, right?"

I nodded. "For a little while. Yes."

"They caught him stealing money from the university. A grand jury indicted him for embezzlement."

"Oh, my god!" I said.

Thirty years later, a police detective contacted me about a student's cold-case rape and murder that had occurred a year before I started working for Tim. Tim was the main suspect. I shared that I recalled a man twice calling the office and angrily demanding to speak with Tim, who, whenever these calls came in, went to his office, shut the door, then emerged looking a bit shell-shocked. "What was that about?" I'd once asked him.

"Just a business deal," he said, shaking his head. The detective did not discount the idea that Tim may have needed money for a payoff to someone who knew too much. Since I'd handled the receivables and payables, I'd possibly complicated a plan to obtain the money and had to be fired. Tim died in 2014, two weeks before an arrest warrant was to be served for the rape and murder. His offer forty years ago to hire someone to kill Kyle remains particularly chilling.

Alcohol continued to hold the enticing denouement for my day. An arrogant manager, maybe an angry human here or there at work, and even a disinterested husband barely fazed me. They just didn't know me as well as wine did. Wine *got* me and understood how I needed to be treated. I needed little else and I behaved. I did my job, paid the bills, cleaned the house, ran errands, read a great deal, smoked a pack a day, and drank. I didn't think much. I didn't feel much.

And then I met with a painting contractor whose bid I needed to review. Wavy blond hair, large blue eyes, and a beautiful smile. He wore shorts the first time I met him, showing off the greatest legs I'd ever seen on a man. The chemistry between us sizzled, so much so that we left the restaurant where we'd met to review the bid and went to my car to talk. "Do you think we'll be able to keep this on a professional level?" he asked.

"No," I said. We leaned into one another and kissed.

Married? Of course. Children? Five. But the toughest hurdle proved to be his Cafeteria Christianity, which allowed him to pick and choose which sins were *real* sins and which could be ignored due to triviality. He said we could kiss and grope, which we did often, but actual intercourse qualified as serious sin. I set out to get him to sin now and ask forgiveness later.

He agreed to meet me at my brother's apartment, where I'd been cat-sitting. We lay down on the bed and started kissing. As soon as I got his pants unzipped and pulled halfway down his thighs, he came all over the side of my head. "Sorry," he said. "I was just so excited!" We got dressed, and I fed the cats. He went back to work, and I drove home—frustrated and unsatisfied once again—with the right side of my hair shellacked in place.

We continued to have lunch together every day, then kiss and touch in my car whenever we could. We had no "sinful" sex, per his definition. He called me one afternoon as I drove home from work. "I really need to see you," he said.

"Oh, tomorrow then. I'm almost home."

"No, I mean I really need to talk to you."

"Can it wait? I'm five minutes from home." Not only five minutes from home, but wine awaited me.

"It won't take long. Just meet me."

I turned around and met him at the property where he'd been contracted to do work for our company. He came over to my car, got in, and turned to me with a smile. "I realized something today," he said. "This could work. We really can have a future together." We agreed to meet for lunch the next day to talk and plan how to make that future happen.

I called Mom a few days later to tell her I'd met someone—although a married someone—and confided that the relationship had grown serious. "You need to come see your mother," she said. I agreed to visit and scheduled a flight.

When Kyle came home from work that evening, he found me on the couch in the den, already ensconced in a buzzed little cocoon of contentment, book in hand, chain-smoking, and drinking wine. Happy, happy, happy. We said hi to one another, then I went back to my book. He stood about ten feet away, watching me. I looked over, shrugged, and tried to resume reading, but he remained, motionless, in my peripheral vision. "You don't need me," he said.

He'd said it so matter-of-factly, he may as well have said we still had plenty of milk left in the refrigerator. Although I'd heard him perfectly well, I wanted him to repeat the words, for they were, to me, a confirmation of a long-fought-for victory over a man who had once regarded me as particularly inept, naive to the ways of the world, too math-challenged to earn more than the most basic of degrees, and so socially awkward that she had to be coached in order for people to like her. A female so unskilled, she needed to be "set up in a boutique," he'd once said, as I supposedly lacked the brains and business skills to do more than sell tchotchkes. And the real topper to the list had been: "Sondra, you'll never find anyone who'll love you like I do."

And so I asked him to repeat what he'd said, for the pure satisfaction of hearing it. "You don't *need* me," he said.

Goddamned straight. "I want a divorce," I said.

He walked over to the sliding glass door and stepped out onto the patio. He slid the door shut behind him and burst into tears. He composed himself quickly and came back in. "Is there someone else?" he asked.

"No. No one," I said.

"Because if there is, you can tell me." He started aimlessly pacing around the room. "There was a woman at work. She really wanted me. She was *really* hot for me," he said, shaking his head, as if amazed by the sheer enormity of her desire.

I couldn't have cared less if he'd had another woman. Or two or three. He'd be their problem. I remained on the couch enjoying my book and wine buzz. He returned a while later and stood in front of me. "There really wasn't another woman," he said.

"I just made it up so you'd feel comfortable telling me if there's another man."

"Okay," I said. *Whatever.*

Exhausted and hungover, I spent most of the next morning at work stretched out on the couch in one of the manager's offices. I dragged my dizzy and nauseated body to meet "my future" for lunch again and to tell him the big news. "Last night, I told Kyle I'm leaving him. It's official now," I said.

His pleasant expression faded. He asked about the particulars of the conversation with Kyle, then spent the rest of our lunchtime a bit reserved. I'd finally taken steps toward a new and hopefully happy future, and the ball rested in his court. His decision involved many more complicating factors than mine: five children, plus business assets to divide. My hangover didn't allow me to worry about much aside from my roiling intestines.

I had flight reservations to see Mom the next week, and I called beforehand to tell her I planned to leave Kyle. "You'd better calm him down before you come to see me," she said. "You don't know what he might pull while you're away."

"Like what?" I asked.

"Like maybe seeing an attorney, filing for divorce, locking you out of the house, getting back at you financially . . . any number of things. And the person who files first usually has better odds in a settlement."

"I didn't think of that," I said.

"So do somethin' to placate him," she said.

The following week, Kyle and I met at Red Lobster for lunch. After we placed our order, I could only stare down at the table and twist my napkin back and forth into a wad. "Just say it," he said.

I couldn't make the words come out. I'd glance up at his pained face, steeled for why I'd asked to meet with him, then return to wringing my napkin. I took another deep breath and exhaled hard. "Could I have another chance?" I asked.

Tears came to his eyes, and he pressed his napkin to his face. "In a heartbeat," he said. "Oh, god. I thought you were going to tell me there's another man."

Nothing outwardly changed between us. We had no celebratory dinner or make-up sex. But I'd accomplished my goal. I could visit Mom with a good amount of confidence that he wouldn't pull anything during my trip.

Time spent with Mom always involved an endless blur of errands. She woke me every morning with a different request. "I need you to keep an eye on the cake in the oven while I shower and get dressed." Or "Get up, honey. I want you to go to the grocery store with me." Or "We've got a lot to do today. Up and at 'em!" The time-zone difference made it difficult for me to fall asleep at night, but I dragged myself out of bed.

She liked to offer me half a sleeping pill before bed to help adjust my sleep schedule but then woke me far too early every morning. "My mother drugs me, then doesn't let me sleep," I told her friends. Mom loved the joke.

We'd leave after breakfast and not return until dinnertime. After eight hours of errands, day after day, my brain and body threatened to crash. On the fourth day, on her patio by the ocean, we finally addressed the real reason for my visit. "His marriage is dead," I said. "She pays him no attention whatsoever."

"That's what all men tell the woman they're havin' an affair with," Mom said. "She's probably a very nice person."

"I'm sick to death of being married to Kyle. Good god, our marriage is so booooooorrrrrrring," I said, crossing my eyes and throwing my head back as if about to pass out.

"Believe me, boring is good," she said. "I know what I'm talkin' about."

I rarely smoked in front of Mom and felt as jumpy and self-conscious as I did back in fourth grade, sneaking cigarettes down at the bayou. I stubbed one out and immediately lit another.

"When are you gonna stop? It's really bad for your skin, and—"

"I know, Mom. I've heard it all before."

"And *five* children? You don't wanna be responsible for breakin' up their home, honey. Those children will *hate* you."

I pondered this as I chain-smoked and pursued a wine buzz. Although a few of Mom's stepchildren had at least treated her with a cool reserve that loosely qualified as respect, she hadn't developed a warm relationship with even one. She'd maintained civility with her current husband's adult daughter, but *adult* was the key word. The five children destined to enter my orbit still lived at home. "They'll blame you for everything," Mom said. "Believe me."

I'd pictured providing fashion advice, makeup lessons, and carefree shopping trips with the four girls. I hadn't yet addressed a relationship with my future stepson. Until the time spent on Mom's patio, I hadn't regarded the children as impressionable, thinking-and-feeling beings whose lives could be nothing short of upended by the choices their father and I were about to make. Although a poster child for the wounds and dysfunction brought on by divorces, I considered no one else's happiness but my own.

"Kyle makes a good living, and he's at least home every night," she added. "And you know, even if you were disfigured somehow, he wouldn't leave you."

I carefully inserted the long nail of my index finger into my wine glass and rescued a drowning mosquito. "Yeah, I guess," I said, flicking him away.

"You've got yourself a good husband," she said.

Back at home, my lover guy's work schedule allowed less time for me than before, and I didn't see him until a few days after my return. The new restaurant we'd chosen for lunch screamed in interior-design agony at a level far greater than the turquoise wonderland ever had. Designed to look like the stereotypical grandmother's house of yore, the result suggested that every yard sale in the state had been hit and relieved of all floral-patterned china in any hue of rose or pink. Even the curtains and chair cushions were variations of pink buds and blooms. Perfect for a *Twilight Zone* scene, the ones in which the room revolved faster and faster to represent the sudden passage of time or told the viewers the characters were being spun off into an alternate reality. Our food appeared, with an unappetizing pallor amid the miasma of rosebuds and pink swirls on our plates. The dizzying number of pattern plays created the sense of movement wherever I attempted to rest my eyes, and I assumed that as a contractor, my "future" must have felt a particularly painful assault on his sense of color coordination. He continued to scan the room and rarely looked at me. The talkative, entertaining man I'd fallen for had turned too reticent for my comfort. When my attempts at making a warmer connection failed, I got to the point. "What do you plan to do?" I finally asked.

He spoke to the rose-patterned wallpaper near our table. "Another time, another place," he said. Apparently, my trip to see Mom had given him time, without the distraction of my presence, to consider what opting for a life with me would cost him, and he decided to dump me.

"Never let a man know he's hurt you." We finished our lunch, then stepped out of the doll house and into reality.

I didn't file for divorce. By then, I had fifteen years invested in the marriage, and I believed my unfulfilling affairs proved that what I sought in a man did not exist. Alcohol enabled me to remain inert and anesthetized within this belief.

He doesn't hit me, run around on me, or call me names.

Vance and his third wife came to town for a short vacation and wanted to get together. He called me at work after they checked into their hotel. "So, are we meeting for dinner tonight?" I asked.

"Well, I want to see you before then," he said.

I looked at my watch. "I'm still at work. It's gonna be a while."

"We don't want to wait. We're just so excited to see you!" he said, in the high-pitched, overly animated voice that had always reminded me of a cartoon puppy. I reluctantly left work and went to see them at their hotel.

Kyle and I met them for dinner that night. Vance also wanted to have dinner with us the following night. And the night after that. By then, the four of us had little left to say to one another. In the car on the third night, I asked what they had planned for the next day, thinking they might do some sightseeing, and I sure as hell didn't want to endure yet another dinner. "We have things *we* want to do," he responded sharply. "We are *not* getting together with you tomorrow."

I told Mom that Vance and his wife had visited. I mentioned our endless dinners and his curt reply to my question. "He was just always so weird," she said.

After he returned to Houston, he sent a note in the mail. "I see a coldness in your marriage with Kyle," he wrote. "Much like the coldness in my marriage to your mother."

Chapter Twenty

After not seeing Mom for over a year and a half, I decided to visit, but this time I asked a friend to go with me. Jane and I had become close when we worked for the same real estate company in Seattle, and I hoped her presence might act as a buffer to my fear of flying, the growing tension in Mom's marriage, and the insane amount of errand running I might avoid. Jane agreed to go. "We're not running errands all day, and we're not going to parties with you every night, Mom. I mean it," I told her. A few weeks before the scheduled trip, Mom filed for divorce.

Almost immediately once we arrived, tension brewed between Mom and Jane. I started running interference, such as when Jane stretched out on one of the silk couches and put her bare feet on it. "You shouldn't have your feet on the couch," I whispered.

"Why? My feet are clean," she said.

"It'll piss Mom off," I said.

"Oh, you can't put your feet on furniture here?" Jane said.

I weenied out yet again about Mom running me into the ground with activity. There we sat one morning, in the car running errands, and we were scheduled to attend a large engagement party for the daughter of one of Mom's friends. Mom shared a bit about her divorce as she drove and filled us in on her soon-to-be ex's reaction to her filing. "So, do you get more money because he's a jerk?" Jane asked.

That night, I put on a short denim dress to wear to the party, then went into Mom's bedroom to talk to her while she finished getting ready. She came out of the bathroom and surveyed me up and down. "Did you bring something else you could wear?" she asked.

I changed into another denim dress, one with longer sleeves and a longer skirt. "Do you have a darker lipstick?" Mom asked. "If you don't, I have some you can borrow," she said. She turned and went to her makeup table without waiting for an answer.

I'd never seen Mom wear a lipstick color outside the spectrum of Creamsicle orange. "Thanks. No thanks," I said.

Her brow furrowed as she continued to study my face, a sure sign that I had not yet passed muster. "And how long have you had that mole on your face?" she asked.

"Since I was born."

"Well, I don't remember it," she said.

"Yeah, you said I was born with it."

"Well, you should have it removed. It's gotten bigger."

I touched the mole on my left cheek to verify. "If you don't remember it, then how do you know it's gotten bigger?"

"Well, I remember it now, and I want you to see a doctor about it when you get home."

Mom, Jane, and I swung by to pick up my brother, who had moved into the area a few years before. Mom tapped the horn and we waited. He came out the front door and walked with his characteristic saunter toward the car.

"Cissie, tell Grey I told him to wear his slacks tonight."

"Mom," I whined. "You tell him."

She called out through my window as it lowered. "Greyson, I specifically told you to wear slacks!"

"I couldn't find 'em," he said, getting into the back seat with Jane.

"Well, where are they?" Mom asked.

"I looked everywhere. Maybe they're at the cleaners," he said.

"Then why didn't you pick them up? You've had plenty of time."

He shrugged. "Just didn't think about it."

Mom drove to the dry cleaners, and Greyson went in to check. "They don't have 'em either," he said, getting back into the car.

We drove back to his apartment. "Go back in there and find them. I said you had to wear slacks."

He came out a few minutes later, still wearing his jeans, and got back into the car. "I found 'em in a pile of clothes in the corner."

"Then why aren't you wearing them?" she asked.

"Can't. My cat peed all over 'em."

Mom's expression went stony, and her mouth remained in a rigid line as she drove us to the party. Greyson and I both wore blue denim. Jane, dressed in cream-colored denim jeans, until then had watched without comment. "Am I underdressed?" she asked.

"No," Mom said coldly. She looked at Greyson in the rearview mirror. "Greyson, I specifically told you to wear your slacks tonight."

"Well, sorry."

We arrived at the party and introductions began. The guest of honor—the soon-to-be bride—wore such a low-cut, see-through dress, she looked as if she'd stepped out of a Victoria's Secret negligee shoot. Greyson, Jane, and I were overdressed in comparison. Mom introduced us to the host of the party—the father of the groom—then walked away to talk to her friends. I left to find wine, then returned to join Mom, Greyson, and Jane, who had found a place to sit among a large group of lawn chairs. I'd missed the first part of the conversation but returned at the moment Mom swiveled in her lawn chair and faced Jane head-on. "Jane, just what is your damned problem?"

"My problem? You want to know my problem?"

"Yeah, I do!" Mom said.

"You're abusive, that's what my problem is!"

Holy shit! I spun around and went to smoke a few cigarettes.

We got home far too late, and far too drunk, and not one of us mentioned the blowup, the remainder of which I'd missed by my retreat. The mood between Jane and me remained chilly the next day as we flew home, and we didn't speak to one another for several months after the trip. Although I did fault her for poor timing and manners, I finally had to admit we all shared blame. She'd witnessed what she believed to be abusive behavior and had the courage to voice it. But I'd grown so used to Mom's constant evaluation of my appearance over the years, it didn't strike me as the least bit odd when she attempted to control what Grey and I wore to a party, even though we were in our forties. If anyone had asked me at the time if I viewed Mom as controlling or abusive, I'd have answered no.

I had little time to think about the trip, because the bank decided to transfer Kyle to Arizona. Fine by me, as I could just as easily drink in Arizona as anywhere. We bought a home in Tucson, and within weeks I was caught up in hundreds of details involving the move. I came to view job transfers as another effective way to tamp down my feelings. I was too busy to process what I felt.

Vance emailed me to tell me his wife had filed for divorce, and I immediately emailed Mom with the news. "Tell him I want him to come visit me," she wrote back. "We're both gettin' a divorce, and maybe we can help each other through."

I called him and extended Mom's invitation. "Please tell her thank you, but I'm still grieving and need time to heal. I'm just not up for it," he said.

Less than a week later, Mom emailed with surprising news. "Vance's on his way to see me," she wrote. He stayed with her for three or four days, and according to both, the visit went exceedingly well. "I'd entirely forgotten how attracted I was to him!" she told me over the phone. She called me every day with details of the blossoming relationship. Vance called me often as well, and every call left me feeling like a conduit for information as to what the other had said.

No matter who spoke to me about the revived relationship, they never failed to mention how I'd worked behind the scenes to get Mom and Vance back together. My grandmother commented on my matchmaking, confused as to why I wanted to see them reunited. "I never did any such thing," I assured her.

"Well, that's not what your mother said."

"Why in the world would I want them back together? They had a terrible marriage," I said.

"My friends just love what you've done!" Mom said.

"Mom, this has to stop. This was not my doing. All I did was relay your message to him."

"I know, but it makes such a cute story!" she said.

"My housekeeper said you must be feeling pretty proud of yourself," Vance told me over the phone.

Their calls to me devolved to the level of elementary school playground talk: "What did he say about me?" and "What else did she say after that?"

I'd reached a new level of frustration when Vance called yet again. "How are you doing?" he asked.

"Pretty good," I said.

"Oh, come on now. You don't have to lie to me," he said. "Your mom told me your marriage is really lacking in intimacy."

So Mom had decided to share personal details of my life. I stopped answering the phone and listened to all messages before returning calls. I stopped acting as a go-between for the two of them and refused to let family members' references to my supposed matchmaking go unchallenged. After a few weeks of the new boundaries, Mom called me in tears. "I just don't feel like you and Greyson are supportive of my relationship with Vance!" she said.

I mumbled placating words. Anything to get her off the phone.

Wine and I had fared so well together. Sure, I'd had my share of hangovers, but I'd also had my share of weeks on end when I didn't drink to what I called excess. Forget the missed days of work, the affairs, the one-night stand in the back of a car and blowing Kyle's best friend at a party. I'd refused to interpret these actions as signs that wine could ever betray me. I'd convinced myself that if I woke without a hangover, I hadn't drunk too much. Then my best friend turned on me. She let me know, under no uncertain terms, that to remain my best friend, she required far more effort from me. Six glasses of wine every night didn't bring the buzz I craved. So I drank more, chasing the warm comfort and assurance I'd received for years but that abruptly and inexplicably eluded me. My best buddy had become quite the spiteful bitch, and with a speed that made her cruelty feel as if it had surfaced overnight. Of course, it hadn't at all; I'd refused to open my eyes.

I decided to try harder. I'd easily adapted over time to polishing off a bottle of wine a night, then a second as the years passed. The thought that I might need to start opening a third bottle alarmed even me.

Upon waking each morning, I gently moved my head to one side to gauge the extent of the pain. I felt lucky if no bowling ball careened through my brain and slammed into the opposite side of my skull. Sick to my stomach, I'd stumble to the bathroom, try not to drop down too hard on the toilet, and then let the diarrhea spew out of me. My complexion bordered on gray, and I'd lost ten pounds I didn't need to lose.

One morning I awoke and couldn't remember a single moment from the previous night. My underwear was missing, and I found it urine-soaked and stuffed between the mattress and the headboard. I stumbled and weaved out to the backyard to check the swimming pool, for it would not have surprised me in the least to find something submerged that did not belong. Fighting the urge to vomit, I made my way back in the house and opened the door to the garage. My car appeared to be fine. I found our schnauzer, Oliver, alive and sleeping comfortably under the covers of our bed.

I racked my brain to remember something, anything, about the previous night. Had Kyle and I fought? I found no note on the kitchen counter or the refrigerator, no hint to warn me that I might be in serious trouble with him. Had I sat in bed and read a book, alone? Did I even speak to him? I made my way to the back of the house to check emails, anticipating a message filled with disgust or anger and closing with "You really fucked up this time." Surely, he'd issue a warning that my days of drinking were numbered. Or else.

Nothing.

I preferred anger to silence. My imagination went wild, and so began an hours-long, paranoid meltdown. I anticipated the worst, for I'd never lost an entire block of time. There was no telling what I might have done. I paced up and down the hallway with clenched fists, hating my bloodshot eyes every time I caught sight of myself in a mirror. *Who is that woman?* My intestines clenched; I ran to the bathroom. With shaking hands, I lit a cigarette in hopes of calming down, but the smell nauseated me. A sip of coffee turned my stomach into a ball of acid.

I despised what I'd become; I didn't know myself anymore. I no longer worked outside the home and had plenty of time to drink. I barely thought or felt after three o'clock every afternoon, a subdued state of being I'd once consciously sought. Although the amount I drank greatly increased, I still did not pay the bills late, let the pool turn green, allow laundry to pile up, or make Kyle come home every night to an empty refrigerator. I kept a pretty yard and an immaculate home.

Desperate to fill my expanding emotional abyss, I'd sought solace from the Church. *Yes, Jesus. Praise Jesus.* Sermons and scripture convicted me: *God didn't give up on you. You can't give up on your husband.* I hadn't. I'd stayed. I'd tried my hardest to find God in church, Sunday school, devotional reading, prayer, Bible study, and Christian speakers on the radio. *"And he walks with me and he talks with me."* I found no fulfillment. It made no sense, and the more I wanted from life, the more my wanting hurt. I'd opted to squelch the pain and stamp out desire, leading to an endless cycle of guilt that screamed for an excess of alcohol, which then resulted in crippling guilt, which screamed for alcohol. *"Be not drunk on wine but be controlled by the Holy Spirit."* Church attendance only lengthened the list of my imperfections and failings, but I hid my addiction to cigarettes and alcohol and feigned reverence and some form of sanity whenever I walked through the doors. *Blessed Assurance, Jesus Is Mine.* But no divine message ever came, nor any sense that an omniscient Being, infinitely more powerful than I, made only of love and forgiveness, gave a single tiny iota of a flying fuck about me.

I opened the bedside table drawer and pulled out a pistol. It had belonged to Dad, and his wife sent it to me after his death. *Why?* I turned it over and over in my hands, trying to recall if I'd ever learned how to use it. *Don't put your finger on the trigger until you're ready.* I thought I recognized the safety but couldn't tell if it was on or off. *What if it's on when I pull the trigger? What if I pull the trigger and the gun isn't loaded?* I admitted I didn't know enough about guns to kill myself with one. I put it back in the drawer and left the bedroom.

Then an email from Kyle came in. Fighting a wave of nausea,

I sat down to steady myself and clicked on the message with a shaky hand.

"Flight delayed. Just checked into hotel. Will call you later. Kiss Oliver for me."

Christ. I'd forgotten all about his San Francisco trip. He wouldn't be home for three days. I sent a calm reply, with no indication of the crisis at home. By three that afternoon, I felt worlds better. I went to the refrigerator and begged my friend to please play nice from then on. I poured a glass and drank.

I walked carefully to the kitchen the next morning, nauseated and dizzy. I held on to the edge of the counter and fought back the urge to vomit. The smell of my sweat and breath disgusted me. I looked upward and no longer cared if there was anyone or anything at all up there to hear me. "I'm not living like this for one more second!" I screamed.

Within a couple of hours, I sat in a large room in Tucson with hundreds of strangers. Attention went from person to person down row after row at table after table. Then all eyes rested on me. My bloodshot eyes filled with tears. "Sondra," I called out. "Alcoholic."

PART III

Chapter Twenty-One

I rarely heard from Mom anymore and called one afternoon in hopes of chatting. "Hey, what's up? I never hear from you."

"Vance and I are in the bathtub," she said.

"Uh . . . I'll just call you back," I said.

"No, that's okay. I can talk now."

I found the visual of them in the tub unsettling, particularly so if she decided to turn the phone over to naked Vance to say hi. "Really, Mom, I'll call back."

"Why did you call?" she asked.

"I miss you," I said, my voice shaking. "We used to talk every day, but now we don't talk at all anymore," I said.

"Well, it is very sorry her is upset. It does not please it for her to cry."

I detested her new habit of referring to us as her and it. "I'll call you some other time," I said, and hung up.

She called the next day. "Are you over whatever it was you were upset about yesterday?"

"No," I said.

"I thought that since you'd gotten it off your chest, you wouldn't be upset anymore."

"Well, I *am* upset. I'll work it out on my own."

She called a few weeks later to say she thought it might be a good time for her to come see me and that my grandmother,

Alma, wanted to visit at the same time. The three of us could finally spend a few days of girl time alone, which we'd never had the opportunity to do. In the past, our focus had been directed at a wedding, funeral, or some other family event. I suggested we have professional photos taken of us to capture the three generations of women together. A couple of weeks before the visit, Mom called. "Vance asked me if he could visit too," she said.

"I don't know about that. That wasn't in the plan at all," I said.

"Well, he really wants to come."

"I'll talk to Kyle about it."

"But Vance wants to go too."

"I'll talk to Kyle and let you know."

"Well, I'm not telling Vance he can't come," she said.

Picking the three of them up at the airport had me white-knuckled enough to consider running into a concourse bar. With only two months of sobriety under my belt, I spent every day feeling as exposed and vulnerable as a snake shedding its skin. When Kyle came home every night, he didn't know if he'd find me crying or baking a cake, my emotions were so fragile.

I met Vance at his gate, and he and I trudged through the sunny, stuffy Phoenix airport to meet Mom's flight, then the three of us went to await the arrival of my grandmother. We had to retrieve luggage for all three of them, at three separate carousels. "God, I want a drink," I mumbled to Mom.

"Well, you can't have one!" she said brightly. "But if you can't drink, then I won't drink either."

On the drive home, my grandmother sat up front with me. Vance and Mom snuggled in the back, blocking my ability to use the rearview mirror. Mom put her coat over the top of their heads and made exaggerated kissing noises. She pushed the coat aside to see if she was getting a reaction out of me. "It's really stuffy in here," I said, adjusting the air vents.

"We know what that means," Vance said, coming out from under the coat.

"Yep. Oh boy," Mom said.

"What?" I asked. "What's strange about my being hot?"

"How old are you?" my grandmother asked.

"Forty."

"You're probably going through the change," she said.

I couldn't live in Arizona and be hot? I shook my head and sighed. It was going to be a long week.

"We sure hope we're not going to be any trouble for you," Vance said.

I looked at him in the rearview mirror. "I hope so too," I said. They took it as a joke and had a good laugh.

Finally at home, I got everyone settled in their bedrooms and went out to the kitchen to slice carrot cake for them. Vance and Mom came around the corner together and took seats at the island. I pushed the plates toward them and handed them forks. Vance took a bite. "This carrot cake is so good," he said.

"Thanks," I said.

"It really is," he said, taking another bite.

"Thanks."

"Mmmmmmm . . . mmmmm . . . mmmm. This might be the best carrot cake I've ever eaten."

"Okay."

"Really, really, really good."

"Thanks."

"It sure is," he said.

Christ, can't this visit just be over already?

"Do you have any wine?" he asked.

Both Mom and Vance knew I had only a few weeks of sobriety under my belt, and I hadn't considered the possibility of them drinking around me. "Uh . . . yeah . . . we have wine," I said.

"Oh, good! I want some too," Mom said. "Mother, do you

want some wine?" she asked my grandmother, who, easily disoriented, had finally found her way to the kitchen from the far end of the house.

"Okay. Just a little, little bit," she said.

We had wine in the house, and Kyle's gin. I'd been advised at my first AA meeting to toss every drop of alcohol we had but couldn't bring myself to do it. Kyle still drank, and much of our wine stash had been business gifts to him. It didn't seem fair to punish him for the sad state I'd gotten myself into. I'd pull myself out of the pit by my fingernails if I had to, but heaven forbid that I inconvenience him. "But I don't want to drink," I'd told the five AAers who counseled me after my first meeting.

They smiled at one another. "If there's no alcohol in the house, you'll have to get in the car and go buy it if you crave it," one of the women said. "That gives you time to think about what you're doing."

"My husband wouldn't like me tossing it all out," I said. There was a lot of headshaking at the AA table. Since then, I'd been so relieved at not being sick and tired all the time, the alcohol in the house hadn't tempted me even once in two months of sobriety. Until the day, that is, when I allowed two of the greatest sources of stress in my life to descend upon my home.

My grandmother proceeded to knock her chardonnay over onto the coffee table. I grabbed paper towels and sopped it up. My senses came to full attention amid the tart, apple-like smell wafting around me. Vance refilled her glass.

"Hey, hey, hey, what's going on here?" Kyle called out, stepping in from the garage.

It's showtime.

He'd already switched into performance mode. I'd memorized the particular act long ago and found his material about as entertaining as "I just flew into town this afternoon. Boy, are my arms tired."

He didn't veer from script and delivered his opening lines at performance volume, loud enough to reach the cheap seats. "What are all these people doing in my house? Hey, Vance, how's it going? Mom! You're looking great. Hey, Alma, don't let these people push ya around, okay? Oh, you're having wine? You want some more? Sondra, get these lushes another bottle! Heh heh heh heh."

"Are you going to be eating dinner with us?" I asked, stepping on his lines at about the one-minute mark.

"I dunno. What are you making?" he asked.

"Salmon," I said, looking at the fillet on the counter. I frowned, noting that Mom had put crushed pecans on it.

"Nah, I'll just make something myself," he said.

I'd set the table in the kitchen, but he soon moved all the place settings to the formal dining room. I picked up the settings and moved them back.

When I woke the next morning and came into the kitchen, Vance and Mom were already up. Vance stood at the stove, dressed only in pajama bottoms, stirring a pan of oatmeal. He stepped in front of me, blocking my way to the coffee, and forced me into a hug. Mom sat at the island, watching us, her eyes all squinty, as if she were about to cry at the sheer beauty of our embrace. Being pressed against his naked chest and stomach felt far too intimate, and I stiffened and pulled away. I took a mug of coffee back to the master bathroom, shut the door, and sat by the sink, firing up cigarette after cigarette.

Mom and Vance had breakfast with my grandmother and me, then spent the rest of the morning holed up in their room. After emerging for lunch, they again disappeared until early afternoon, when they came out to the living room and announced their plan to leave for Sedona the next day. This required me to take them to pick up a rental car. Before they left the next morning, I drew a map of the most direct route for their drive. Five or so minutes after I thought they'd driven off, I looked out and saw them in the car, still in the driveway. Vance rolled down the window when I approached. They had a state map of Arizona spread open before them. "We can't figure out how to get there," he said.

"I gave you easy directions, though. I wrote it out," I said.

"Kyle told us to go a different way."

"Well, I guess you'll have to ask him then," I said, shrugging.

They drove off, leaving my grandmother behind with me. "It's just so odd they'd up and leave," she said. I took her to the mall, then to lunch at a neighborhood bookstore that had an aviary built into one of the walls. Our shared intense love of birds bordered on reverence, and we sat together silently and watched them.

Mom and Vance returned from Sedona the next day. She mentioned they'd gotten lost shortly after leaving our house the day before and had driven in circles for over an hour. They took their bags to the back bedroom and shut the door, then reappeared in the den late that afternoon, right on schedule. "Could we open some wine?" he asked.

Vance had reminded me several times of an opera performance he wanted to see on cable, and I spent an exceedingly long time trying to find it. He'd started to lose his hearing and required the volume to be turned up high. Just as he and Mom got situated on the couch and tenor voices blared, Vance fell asleep with his head back and mouth wide open. Whenever Mom or I tried to adjust the volume of the singing, it woke him. He soon tired of watching, and he and Mom disappeared into the back bedroom again.

I hadn't had even a minute alone with Mom, so when I found her in the hall bathroom removing her makeup that evening, I went in, jumped up on the counter, and started chatting. She said little, and her movements were so rushed as to be almost frantic. She flossed and brushed her teeth, then turned and left the bathroom. "Good night!" she called out as she shut her bedroom door.

At five thirty the next morning, I went to the kitchen table and drew a map for Vance to follow to get to the airport. A massive ongoing construction project had made getting to the airport much more difficult than usual, so I made sure the directions were precise, even crumpling up some of the attempts and starting over. When Vance came into the kitchen, I handed the directions to him. "This should get you there in one piece," I said.

"Thanks, but Kyle's going to show us how to get there."

As soon as they drove off, I strode to the back of the house and stripped off all the sheets and pillowcases with such force, it's a wonder I didn't tear them. I tossed it all into a pile in the hallway. I threw every towel and washrag they'd used on top of the mass. I lugged it all down the hall, hurled it onto the utility room floor, and slammed the door.

I showered and dressed and made it to a seven o'clock AA meeting. When I came home, I started cleaning. By noon, every trace of their visit had been erased from my house.

Soon, both Mom's and Vance's divorces were final, yet they didn't marry one another immediately. Apparently, tension brewed with Vance's daughter, who expressed concern that he might be hurt again should he decide to reunite with Mom. Mom emailed to update me on the growing drama:

"All that stuff I went through with Vance was a long time ago, and it's time to move on. She needs to just get over it."

Bells, alarms, and whistles fired off in my head. Without giving myself time to chicken out, I fired back a response. "Well, I have to tell you, children don't just get over divorces. I haven't 'just gotten over' your actions after all these years and will forever struggle to understand your choices. I find so much of what you do infuriating."

She responded that she didn't know whether to be hurt or angry at what I'd written.

Bombs away. I fired off a four-page letter about bringing Vance without my approval, then spending no time with me; about prioritizing shopping for jewelry over having lunch with me when she came to Los Angeles; and about not protecting Greyson and me by standing up to Dan. She never saw what an angry and abusive man he was? Bullshit! I demanded to know why she never ordered him to stop beating her children with a belt. After a few more pages of vented resentments, I told her that what I'd always wanted to hear her say was "I'm sorry."

She responded that she was pained to learn that I still held such resentment, and to please not tell her when she's ninety-five that I'm still angry. She wanted me to let go of the past. She said she was glad Dan came along when he did, because she didn't know how she could have supported Greyson and me without him, and that if I'd had children of my own, I might understand. She wrote a great deal about her mother and her struggle to raise her and Lu without a husband. She summarized by saying she hoped she'd learned from the past so she could do better in the future.

And still no apology.

When she and Vance decided shortly thereafter to remarry one another, she informed me that a few ministers they'd consulted refused to perform the ceremony. Counting the upcoming nuptials, Vance and Mom had ten marriages between the two of them, and few denominations cared to bless serial marriage. The Catholic Church was certainly out. After scouting about for a while, they found a willing Episcopalian priest. "He told us, 'In the eyes of God you two are still married anyway,'" Mom said, her voice breaking with emotion. If so, they were both still married to quite a few people.

Chapter Twenty-Two

I believed cigarettes had helped me achieve three months of sobriety. They helped me shove down my feelings. I'd tried to stop smoking and drinking at the same time but heard voices, a cacophony that can only be described as several people endlessly whispering to me. I started therapy with a Christian counselor through my church and continued to smoke, since it silenced the voices. Finally, I knew the time had come to quit. I'd heard of success with Wellbutrin, an antidepressant that had the off-label effect of reducing nicotine cravings. At my upcoming annual physical, I asked my doctor about a prescription. "Sure. Anything to get you to quit smoking," she said, listening to my heart. "Are you sexually active?" she asked while pressing around on my stomach.

"No, I'm married," I said.

She laughed and continued with the exam. A few moments later, her expression became serious. "What you just said about sex. Did you mean that?"

I put my hands over my face and started to cry. "My marriage is dead. It's always been dead. We haven't had sex for over a year."

She presented a weak little speech about how married couples were supposed to have sex. As if I were a wife who did not know this. "Well, let's get two birds with one stone here, okay? I'll prescribe Wellbutrin for your smoking but also for your general mood. And I want to see you back here in a few months to check on how you're doing."

I left with a prescription, dropped it off at the pharmacy, then went home. Kyle came in from work a short while later and found me teary-eyed. I went into the bedroom with him, and while he changed his clothes, I told him about the conversation with the doctor.

"Is the sex problem so bad you would divorce me over it?" he asked.

"No, no. I would never do that," I said.

While paying bills one afternoon in our home office, I decided to clean out the desk. One of the envelopes in the bottom drawer contained receipts for cash requests made at the nearby casino. Kyle and I used to play slot machines together quite often, but I'd long ago stopped enjoying it, and, as far as I knew, so had he. A few trips to the casino without me weren't a concern, but the sheer number of cash withdrawal receipts I held in my hand floored me. I turned to the computer on the console behind me and started an Excel spreadsheet. I went to the hall closet, dug through all the pockets in his golf bag, and found yet another handful of receipts. By the time I finished adding the amounts to the spreadsheet, the result was staggering, and there was no telling how many more cash withdrawals there might have been. He'd gambled and lost more money than most people make in an entire year.

When he walked in the door that evening, his steps slowed when he saw the stack of yellow receipts on the table in front of me. "I need to talk to you," I said. He stopped near the kitchen and came no closer. "I found these this afternoon," I said with a shaky voice. He remained silent, staring at the stack, then back at me. "I added it all up. This is fifty thousand dollars of losses," I said.

He didn't look at all surprised, but he did look ashamed. "I asked for a summary at the casino a few weeks ago. I saw the total and couldn't even believe it myself," he said. I didn't ask him what that total was. "I'll stop going. I really will," he said. We left it at that.

A few weeks later, while cleaning the area around the hearth, I found a small piece of yellow paper with charred edges under the fireplace grate. Another casino cash request receipt. My mind went into overdrive to figure out the source of all the withdrawals. I saw all the monthly bills, and I paid them from our joint account. He traveled often, so cash advances and reimbursements flew back and forth throughout the month, and I'd never paid them much mind. There had to be something I'd overlooked. I went to the filing cabinet in our home office and thumbed through the financial folder. I rarely opened the large envelopes that arrived each month from the investment company; I'd always left financial planning to Kyle. But each envelope had been opened, and the monthly statements were incomplete. I called the financial adviser on our account and requested duplicates of the missing pages. "That's odd," she said. "Your statements are always missing pages?"

"Strange, huh? If you could just resend the past few months maybe," I said.

Kyle came home a few days later and wasted no time as soon as he came through the door. "I can't believe you'd embarrass me this way!" he said.

"What? What did I do?" I asked.

"I got a call about missing pages on our financial statements. I didn't know you'd requested them. You made me look like an idiot!"

"Well, I found a burned casino receipt in the fireplace a few days ago. Talk about not being very smart," I said.

"Well, maybe if I had more support around here, I wouldn't feel the need to gamble," he said.

"Oh, please," I said, rolling my eyes. "I have my own addictions. No way am I taking on yours."

A few minutes later I went to the back of the house and saw him heading toward the hall bathroom, holding a small stack of papers. Even from several feet away, I could tell by the size of the pages and the print layout they were from our financial statements. "I want to see those, Kyle."

He sped up his pace, went into the bathroom, and shut and locked the door. I waited in the hallway for him to finish whatever he planned to do within. When he came out, he had no papers.

"Give them to me, Kyle."

"Drop it. Just drop it," he said, continuing down the hallway toward the den.

I went in, sat down on the floor, and opened the cabinets beneath the sink. He kept several stacks of golf magazines there, and I felt certain the missing sections had to be hidden somewhere within their pages. After thumbing through countless issues and failing to find the evidence, I gave up. But the duplicate pages I received from our financial adviser provided all the proof I needed: he was gambling, and losing, our investments.

Cinco de Mayo 2003. After being on Wellbutrin for two weeks, I returned all my unopened packs of cigarettes to Walgreens. The new, smokeless me stepped on the bathroom scale each morning, registered disbelief, stepped off, gave the scale time to reset, then stepped on again in hopes of discovering a malfunction. Coincidentally, a marketing letter arrived in the mail from a personal trainer, and Kyle said one of his business associates had good things to say about the studio. I booked an appointment with Drake, the owner, for the next morning.

Oh my god, what a physique. Oh my god, oh my god, oh my god. The pull of the testosterone wafting around this man. He looked even better during the second workout, wearing a skin-tight black shirt that defined every muscle in his chest, stomach, and back. The size and rock-hard definition of his upper body fascinated me, and I struggled to keep from staring—or worse, touching him. After our third session together, I could bear it no longer. "What would you charge to let me feel those muscles?" I asked, pointing to his chest. I tried to make it sound like a joke.

"I might let you do that. You'd have to be respectful about it, though."

In the middle of my next workout, he stepped in front of me, looked me square in the eye, and took hold of my wrists. "I'll let you touch me," he said, placing my palms on his chest. The feel of his muscles turned electric. Sexual. I pulled my hands away.

I increased my workout schedule to four times a week. No junk food whatsoever; no cigarettes, liquor, or even sugar. The sex drive shoved down under decades of booze, nicotine, and marital resentment came roaring back like a freight train. The chemistry between Drake and me was undeniable. Palpable. And mutual. But no matter where I looked for validation, the odds never came up in favor of an affair to result in a happy, committed relationship. My own history should have pounded this knowledge hard and deep within my brain: I was most likely, yet again, on the Affair Road to Failureville. But god, I wanted to be touched. More than anything, I wanted to be wanted.

We scheduled our first rendezvous at Drake's place one night when Kyle was out of town on business. He let me in the front door, then excused himself and went to the kitchen. I'd expected his home to be decorated in oversized leather furniture resting on bearskin rugs. He'd have subdued lighting, a roaring fire, and quiet music playing on the stereo. Instead, I walked into minimalistic and contemporary decor in black, red, and white.

"Sorry, but I haven't eaten in a while," he called out. I followed the sounds of a pinging microwave. We silently watched his Lean Cuisine dinner revolve in its little tray. I wondered how such a muscular man fared with such a tiny meal, especially given what we were about to do. I waited as he stood, bent over his food on the counter, and ate his dinner. When he finished, he came out of the kitchen and walked toward the couch. "Take off your clothes and lie down," he said, pointing.

So, this is how it's going to be? I ended up naked on the couch in a weird, twisty kind of position, with my head in the corner and my body angled outward off the edge to accommodate him, as he apparently intended to remain standing. His left arm was on the back of the couch, and his right arm was on the armrest, placing him far above me. He didn't kiss me, there was no foreplay, and . . . oh god, not again.

Another spongy-soft penis, barely able to enter me. He looked at the wall behind the couch, rarely glancing down. He continued to pump, and each powerful thrust of his hips slammed my head against the inside corner of the sofa. "Has anyone ever made love to you like this before?" he asked the wall.

"Um, no."

He continued to pump, but with no improvement on the horizon. "Let's move to the bedroom," he suggested.

"Sure, yeah."

I lay down on the bed and activities resumed. After several minutes, his erection hadn't progressed, although he continued to thrust hard against me. I checked out and studied the ceiling. *Not a popcorn ceiling at least. I hate those. Four blades on the ceiling fan. Which way are the blades supposed to turn for winter? Have I ever changed the direction on mine?*

He got hard momentarily and came. He remained on top of me for a while, leaving more time for me to observe the decor. There were black, satiny throw pillows on the bed with little white martini glasses on them. His black-and-white robe hung on the bathroom door. I pictured him at Target, thumbing through robe after robe until he found one that would match. The closet doors were mirrored, so I sneaked peeks at him lying motionless on top of me. His muscles were so large, I couldn't see myself under his bulk. He rolled off and made his way to the bathroom. "Sorry about that," he called out over his shoulder. "I was nervous. It'll be better next time."

The disappointment of the previous evening didn't tamp down the physical chemistry between us as I'd anticipated. My workouts with him had always been erotic, and our time together the next morning in the studio proved to be no exception. The simplest of touches from him were processed by my body as sexual. His hands on my waist as he positioned me properly in front of equipment. The feel of him as he stood behind me, his hard chest pressed against my back. When he held my hips gently and patted them, telling me "Good job" after a set. Or when his strong hands came from behind, making their way up my stomach to caress my breasts. When his fingers stroked me through the material of my workout shorts or made their way inside. No matter how he touched me, my body responded to the sensations as foreplay, maintaining my libido at slow burn. If I wasn't with him, I wanted to be. If he wasn't touching me, I wanted him to immediately. If my mind wasn't spinning a sexual fantasy about him, it soon would be.

I sat down on the mat, and he guided me through stretching exercises that signaled the end of my hour with him. His favorite started with me on my hands and knees, and on follow-through had my chest on the ground and my tailbone in the air. Whenever I assumed this pose, he stepped around to view me from behind. This time, he walked to the front door and locked it. He unzipped his pants. I lay down on my back and slipped out of my shorts, hurling them to the side. As he lowered himself on top of me, I took hold of his shoulders and pulled him hard against my chest as he thrust inside.

He was as hard as a steel pipe. I wrapped my legs around his waist and my arms around the massive muscles in his back and held on as the force of his thrusts rocked me back and forth. There was nothing about him in that moment that was anything but powerful and masculine. The smell of his skin and sweat intoxicated me. The bristle of his unshaven face brushed against my cheek with each thrust.

My hands moved up and down the length of his back, exploring every rise and ripple of his shoulders, then stroking the muscles that tapered toward his waist. I kissed his face, his ears, his neck and shoulders as his pace became more forceful and fervent. The bulk of his biceps under my palms felt safe and protective.

He further swelled within me. I pulled his hips against mine, wanting him as deep inside as possible. The slick and silky heat. He shuddered again and again. Then a moan. He lowered himself on top of me. His breath was fast-paced and warm on my neck. We remained in each other's arms for a while.

I knew I could never return to life as usual. At forty-four years old, I finally learned, flat on my back on a dirty gym mat, just what the fuss over sex was all about. As I held him and stroked the back of his head, a message resonated: *This is what you've been searching for, for as long as you can remember. And this is the man who will give it to you.*

I went home, called Mom, and burst into tears. "I'm so tired of pretending I have a happy marriage. I want to divorce Kyle."

She didn't seem surprised. "Look, I'm not sayin' you shouldn't leave him, but at least get yourself a good therapist first."

"I'm already in counseling through the church."

"Well, what does your counselor say?"

"I'm supposed to continue praying for God to heal my marriage."

"Well, how the hell long are you supposed to pray? Find yourself a therapist, and I mean a really good one. And stay away from the Christians."

"Okay. God, I just don't want to hurt Kyle," I said.

"He'll get over it."

"Yeah. Maybe," I said.

"And pull together all your financial information. Do it without Kyle knowing. You gotta start thinkin' like a man," she said.

Three days later, I sat in my new therapist's office. It was a tiny room, only big enough for a love seat, an overstuffed chair, and a roll-top desk off in the corner. The large glass picture windows—one beside me and one behind her—were tinted to block the Arizona sun, but so much so that the world outside appeared as if winter had already moved in. In fact, summer approached, and small cactus gardens were in view from my side of the room. I immediately felt comfortable with the surroundings but wasn't sure about the therapist yet. I didn't get any kind of first impression "hit" of connection or trust as I had with others. She was elegant in posture and dress and spoke with an Italian accent. She struck me as a bit cool and sealed-off. There were other therapist options if she wasn't a good fit, so I took the plunge with a condensed history, a rambling "I don't feel this, he did this, I said that, we don't have sex, then he said, then I said, and I want out, but I don't want to hurt him, and it's been twenty-three years and—"

She held up a palm to silence me, leaned forward in her chair, and laced her fingers together. "Sondra, if you don't have an emotional, spiritual, or sexual connection with your husband after twenty-three years, you are never going to. You emotionally divorced this man a long, long time ago."

Bam.

Finally, a therapist who didn't think all they needed to do

was get Kyle and me to have sex. She didn't believe we needed marriage counseling. No, it was far, far too late for that. "If you stay, you become a martyr. If you stay, you will never again find the courage to leave," she said.

A few days later, while waiting at an intersection for the traffic light to change, a heavy wave of sadness came over me. I was headed home and knew with all certainty that the last place I wanted to be was in my loveless house. I saw myself gratefully flipping burgers and willingly living in a dark, dank apartment for the rest of my days if that were the cost—anything to avoid living one more day in my dead marriage. Somewhere along the way, despite all the self-defeating decisions, rationalizations, affairs with married men, numerous half-hard penises, and sense-deadening haze of alcohol and cigarettes, I finally realized I was a woman who had a lot going for her. And my therapist was no doubt correct: if I changed my mind this time, I would never again be able to summon the courage to leave.

I picked up my ringing cell phone and saw Drake's studio number displayed. "She was just here. She went into my apartment, snooped around, and found your lingerie and the Victoria's Secret receipt with your name on it. She came into the studio and threw all of it in my face," he said.

"She" was Tamara, Drake's ex-girlfriend. He'd interpreted her move-out from his apartment weeks prior and the return of his key as the end of their relationship. She apparently did not share his opinion.

"Oh, god. Oh god, oh god, oh god, oh god," I said.

"She *will* call Kyle. I promise you that," he said.

Kyle was due back from a business trip the next afternoon. What if she called him before he got home? What if she'd already called him? "Oh, god."

"I'm sorry, baby," he said.

"I have to finally face it," I said.

"I'm so sorry," he said. "She'd given back my key but had made a duplicate, obviously. I just got back from my place. She tore up my magazines and squirted whipped cream all over the mirrors."

It was easy to put the pieces together. Weeks before, she'd shown up unannounced at the studio, ostensibly to work on Drake's books and do his bank deposit as she'd done while they'd dated. I was near the front door, warming up on a treadmill, and could easily see her reflection in the windows. She turned her back to me and put on lipstick before greeting Drake at the rear of the studio. She returned to the front office and began scrolling through a list on the computer, and her stony expression showed she was on a mission. She at some point pulled up my name and personal information, which included Kyle as an emergency contact—not only his cell number but our landline at home.

When the treadmill timer went off, I stepped into the office and, without a word of greeting to her, put an empty water bottle into the recycling bin. She remained in the studio for my hour-long session. I watched them as Drake went out to the parking lot with her afterward. Before opening her car door, she turned to him, leaned up, and kissed him on the mouth. I was envious that her lips had touched his. Drake came back into the studio and said she had scolded him. "You shouldn't be so personal with your clients," she'd said.

"Don't tell me how to do my job," he'd replied.

For Tamara, it had all begun to add up. Drake's interest in her had waned substantially. She'd moved out of his apartment a few weeks before, finding one she could afford on her own on the far side of town. He'd helped her get established, had even helped her get a job, but it was obvious, he said, the relationship wasn't going anywhere. What little remaining connection they had with one another had been abruptly severed when I appeared on the scene.

Anyone who saw the two of us together could surely see the chemistry, and our sessions in his studio were chatty and flirtatious. He no longer showed interest in Tamara's days, much less her nights. And although usually interested in sex, he no longer moved on her. Having been cheated on by her ex-husband, she knew the signs. "I want my apartment key back," Drake had told her. When she placed it in his palm a few days later, he thanked her.

She'd come into the studio unexpectedly again—I noted that she somehow knew my workout schedule—and stayed on the treadmill throughout, turning and stealing furtive glances at us in the mirrors that lined almost every wall. "She's watching us!" I'd whispered to Drake.

He looked back over his shoulder and shrugged. "Whatever," he said.

He'd received two hang-up calls at the studio the next day. After making sure he was there, not at home, she drove to his place, went to his front door, and slipped her duplicate key into the lock.

His rigid insistence on neatness and order left only the barest signs that anyone occupied the apartment. Living with him had been twenty-four hours a day of walking on eggs, she'd told him. There would be no extra coffee cup in the sink, or any obvious hints of someone else having been there. If she scanned the living area and den, she'd find nothing out of place. In his closets, the clothes hung in perfect lines, divided by category. Slacks with slacks, dress shirts with dress shirts, evenly spaced and facing the same way. He only used white plastic hangers, for he detested wire hangers. "No more wire hangers ever!" she'd once joked.

She went to the bureau at the far wall and began rifling through each drawer. Upon opening the bottom left one, she found several pairs of my silky thongs and a red-and-black sheer negligee trimmed in lace. Buried under all of it, my Victoria's Secret receipt. She went to the spare bathroom at the front of the apartment and tore up all of Drake's magazines, hurling the pages throughout the living area. She took whipped cream from the refrigerator and squirted it wherever a mirror hung: above the chest of drawers, above the leather couch in the den, and in both bathrooms. For good measure, she hurled the throw pillows from his bed and couches onto the floor. Taking all the lingerie with her, she left the apartment and drove to Drake's studio, where she found him in the front office talking to a client. "These belong to your cheatin' whore!" she yelled. She threw the lingerie in his face and left. Drake called me immediately.

I had about twenty-four hours to stew in fear over my infidelity and face the self-hate that came from not having gone ahead and filed for divorce. The landline phone rang later that afternoon. When I answered, my stomach lurched at the sound of Kyle's voice. His tone and banter told me Tamara had not called him. Yet. I woke in the middle of the night, and within seconds the overwhelming dread returned. I lay staring at the ceiling. *What have you done? What have you done? What have you done?*

What had I done? I'd gotten caught, that's what I'd done. *Stupid. You stupid, stupid girl.* I knew I'd be awake all night, cursing myself for not having the courage to up and leave decades ago. *Because you're weak and afraid. Afraid of everything. You make me sick.*

I pictured the devastation in Kyle's eyes, his disbelief that I could be so dishonest. But no matter what happened, I planned to leave him. If the future included Drake, all the better; I adored him. But I knew my marriage was over.

I spent the next day at home, by myself, waiting. My brain continued its wild and endless stream of possible scenarios that might unfold once Kyle found out about the affair. I could no longer buffer my fear or any other unpleasant emotion with alcohol or cigarettes. This mess had to be faced head-on and demanded the use of a sober mental muscle that had sat, unused, since I'd first listened to the voice in my kitchen, the gentle and assuring whisper that told me alcohol was the answer.

Around five o'clock, I heard the familiar rumble and creak of the garage door. I went to help Kyle bring in his luggage from the car and studied his body language and expression. So far, so good. But as soon as we finished bringing all his bags into the house, the phone rang. *Don't answer it, don't answer it, don't answer it.*

He walked over and picked up the landline in the kitchen. "This is Kyle," he said. The set of his expression and the protracted silence as he listened told me it was Tamara. I remained by the pantry door, frozen in place, watching. "Yeah, I suspected that too," he said. He listened for a short while longer. "Call me this week, and we can talk more about it." He gave her the number for his direct line at the bank, then hung up. I followed him down the hall toward our bedroom, each of us carrying luggage. The large mirror by the front door reflected the face of a man who looked as if he'd just been kicked in the stomach. He went into the master bedroom closet and started changing out of his work clothes.

"Who was it?" I asked, standing at the closet door.

"Just the golf course, wanting to talk to me about my membership," he said.

"On a Friday night?" I asked.

"Yeah." His shoulder hit mine squarely as he strode past me. He took his cigarettes and lighter and went out to the patio that bordered the back of the house. I followed him outside and sat down in what had been our shared smoking area for years. He lit a cigarette and stared at the nearby cactus-covered hills. "She said you were with him last night," he said.

It might have helped me fabricate a good story had I asked who "she" was. Who the hell cared what she said about me? The jig was up. But I was still so scared of coming clean, I insisted on defending myself against accusations that no longer even mattered. "How could I have been with him last night?" I said. "When you called, I was home. I mean, you called on the landline even. How could I have faked—"

"She said she's been following you the past few days. She said you drive a red Mustang, and—"

"But I don't drive a—"

"Yes, I know that, Sondra. She sounds like a desperate woman. Like someone coming unhinged." He continued to smoke his cigarette and stare off into the distance. "Have you been sleeping with this man?" he asked.

"No, but I want to," I said. I took a deep breath. "I don't want to be married anymore, Kyle."

Once I spoke the words, I wasn't scared anymore—not scared of the uncertainty, not scared of a future without him, not scared of his anger or silent treatment. It was one of the most beautiful and freeing moments of my life. No more charades. No reason to sneak around. No need for lies from that point forward. No more pretending I could endure the marriage for the rest of my days. "I don't want to be married anymore."

He stared off into the distance, looking as if he were running a complicated math calculation in his head. I stood and reached out to hug him. "I can't," he said, holding his arm out to keep me at bay. I sat back down and waited. "But we have what everyone wants," he said. "We have the American Dream. We have money, and you don't have to work, and—"

I shook my head. "I just had my forty-fourth birthday. And I get lonelier and lonelier every year," I said.

"But we can get counseling. We can go to therapy together again."

"We've already done that," I said, waving the idea away with my hand. "And I've gone to therapy alone as well."

"Well, the bank sure isn't going to like this," he said. "They like stable people."

He stopped speaking to me, and I moved into the guest bedroom that night.

Neither one of us moved out immediately. We attempted to live amicably in the house together until we hammered out the details of the divorce. I started searching for a place to live. A few weeks later, after Kyle came home from work one evening, I went to the door of the master bedroom closet to talk to him as he changed clothes. "I'm gonna need a down payment for a townhome I want to buy," I said.

"That's fine," he said, shrugging.

"I mean, I'll need it soon. Will that be a problem?"

"No. Should be fine." I turned to leave the bedroom but stopped when he spoke. "I can see it now," he said. "In five years, you'll be in your third marriage. You're going to turn out just like your mother."

I walked away, leaving his words hanging in the air between us.

"You might consider not seeing Drake until your divorce is final," my therapist said.

"There's no way. No way," I said.

"Has Kyle gotten angry yet?" she asked.

"Not what I'd call angry, really. All things considered."

"I assure you, he'll get angry. And your divorce and settlement will probably proceed more easily if there isn't another man in the picture. Kyle can use Drake as leverage. Why not tell Drake you can't see him until the divorce is final?"

Inconceivable. "I won't do it," I said, shaking my head.

"A long-standing marriage and a pretty wife made Kyle look normal, Sondra, when he is anything but. He's not only terrified of being alone, he fears the real Kyle will now be exposed."

But if Kyle's anger or fear propelled him to play dirty in divorce court, my ace in the hole would be his decades-long sexual rejection of me. And I knew with all certainty, Kyle knew this. I didn't give a rat's ass what he might try to pull or what he might be going through emotionally. Without a single doubt, I believed I'd earned my way out of the marriage.

I continued to live at the house while waiting to close on my townhouse. Kyle started going to clubs at night in hopes of meeting women, leaving me free to see Drake more often. My divorce experience was most likely one of the happiest on record, and I told my therapist of my mother's reaction: "If I'd known you were going to be so happy," Mom had said, "I never would have convinced you to stay married."

My therapist studied me for a moment, then sat forward in her chair, a movement that never failed to warn of something particularly weighty coming my way. "Sondra, you let your mother decide if you stayed married? Why do you give her such control over you?" I could only offer a blank stare. "Sounds to me like you have a lot more to work on here than just your divorce."

As I ate a small breakfast before leaving to work out with Drake, a dull pain twinged in my lower right side. Thinking it was only a passing cramp, or maybe something period-related, I didn't pay it much mind. Swallowing a bite of scrambled eggs brought on a wave of nausea. For a while, I sat with the twinges, which quickly turned to waves of pain. I called my neighbor. "I need to go to the emergency room," I said.

Within an hour, the pain felt like a gasoline-fueled fire in my abdomen. An ultrasound revealed an orange-sized teratoma on my right ovary, a growth so large and heavy, it had caused torsion and cut off circulation. Emergency surgery was scheduled to remove the ovary and fallopian tube. My neighbor let

Drake know where I was, and she notified Kyle, who was out of town on business. Drake rushed to the emergency room, and I got to spend a few minutes with him before being taken upstairs. "Remember all of our plans," he said. "All the things we want to do together. I love you."

Late that afternoon, Kyle rushed into my hospital room. He looked at the catheter line and bag of my pee attached to the side of the bed and grimaced. "Ewwwww. That's gross," he said. He was fidgety but oddly upbeat, smiling as he paced the length of the far wall in front of me. I hadn't seen him smile in weeks, and we hadn't spoken more than a few words to one another since I'd told him I planned to file for divorce. "God, I hate hospitals," he said.

"I get released tomorrow morning, I think."

"I left the meeting so fast, I didn't even check out of my hotel," he said.

For the past year or so, I could barely stand to be in the same room with him. His presence had drained me of energy and created the sensation of air being sucked out of a room. The lines and monitors held me captive, forcing me to remain in place as he paced back and forth at the end of my bed. I grew agitated by his self-involved chatter. He needed to leave. "Drake will probably come to visit this evening," I said.

His edgy smile disappeared. He went to the whiteboard on the far wall and wrote his name and phone number under Contact Information. With tear-filled eyes, he walked out.

As soon as I could walk without pain, I moved into my new townhouse. I called Kyle a few days later to tell him I planned to pick up the remaining things I'd left at the house. Instead of being at work when I arrived, he'd stayed home. I found him attempting to vacuum the living room, but the vacuum kept shorting out. "Why don't you take this one and I'll go buy a new one? Then I don't have to mess with getting it repaired," he said. I ignored the question. No longer my problem.

He stood in the driveway and watched me load my car. "Why is it taking you so long to get your stuff?" he called out as I started to back out of the driveway.

I stopped and rolled the window down. "I didn't think it was. I was in the hospital."

"This just can't go on," he said.

"Well, I didn't exactly plan the tumor."

"I left a meeting with my most important client and rushed back here to the hospital because of you," he said.

"But I didn't plan to end up in the emergency room."

He turned and started walking toward the house.

"I said I didn't do it on purpose!" I yelled at his back.

He disappeared into the garage.

"Do you hear me?" I called out.

Chapter Twenty-Three

As soon as Mom and Vance laid eyes on Drake at the airport, I knew they didn't like him. Tepid smiles, perfunctory handshakes, and a quiet ride in the car. Drake attempted to make conversation, but their responses sounded bored and unenthusiastic. We stopped for lunch at a steak house, and they treated Drake politely enough as we ate but showed no interest in getting to know him.

I'd never seen the home Mom and Vance bought after they remarried. I noted that Mom and I had unknowingly chosen the same exact granite—hers in the kitchen and mine for our master bath. Drake and I were shown to the downstairs guest bedroom. When I came back upstairs, Vance asked if I wanted to go with him to the grocery store to rent some videos. He didn't speak for the first few minutes as he drove. "I've got something to say," he said. "I don't know how to say it, so I'm just going to put it out there."

"Okay," I said.

"What's your financial arrangement with Drake? What does he pay to live with you?"

"Sometimes he pays me more, sometimes he pays me less," I said.

"Well, that doesn't sit well with me. It doesn't sit well with me at all."

Vance, a retired doctor, lived in one of the most exclusive areas of the state, yet stopped to top off his gas tank when he spotted a price at a few cents less a gallon. He kept meticulous records of monthly expenditures and required Mom to pay exactly half. Drake's income as the owner of a personal training studio fluctuated. He paid me half of what he earned each month, but it varied. Annoyed with myself for answering Vance's question, I didn't respond further.

Hurricane Frances had first made landfall several days before in Florida, then moved into the Gulf of Mexico, then made landfall again and headed north. Still, I hadn't changed our flight reservations because she was well south of us and we planned to stay only a few days. So far, all we'd seen of her in the first few hours of our visit was steady, moderate rain. Vance and I rode home from the grocery store in a heavier downpour.

The four of us gathered around the television to watch *Girl with a Pearl Earring*. About five minutes in, the lights flickered, came back on, flickered again, then went dark. No power, so no air-conditioning or lights. No running water.

We did okay roughing it the first night. Mom lit numerous candles, and we ate salmon prepared on the patio grill. Drake and I used a flashlight to navigate our way to and from our basement bedroom and were in pitch darkness by the time we went to bed. The rain slammed hard against the roof.

I came upstairs early the next morning, hoping against hope Mom had a way to make coffee without electricity. She did have a French press and successfully prepared a cup for me, although it came out lukewarm. "So, how is it that Drake can afford a new car and motorcycle?" she asked as she moved around the kitchen.

"What? What are you talking about?"

"Well, at dinner he mentioned you two riding his motorcycle to Sedona. And he also said something about the new car he bought."

"He already had a motorcycle. Only the car is new," I said.

"Well, how can he afford it if he doesn't work?"

"Who said he doesn't work?" I asked. "He's the only one out of the four of us in this house who *does* work."

Mom turned to me, holding a spatula, which she used for emphasis as she spoke. "Well, I have to tell you, Vance and I sat up very late last night discussing this. We believe Drake is taking advantage of you."

"How the hell could he be taking advantage of me?" I said, my voice rising. "Christ, he pulled in six figures last year in his studio."

"I just knew if I said anything at all about this to you, you'd go absolutely bonkers," she said.

"Do you see anything in my demeanor right now that says I'm going absolutely bonkers?" My eyes stung, threatening tears, and the cup in my hand shook. *Don't you dare cry. Don't you even think about it.*

"Well, I wish when I was your age someone had warned me about being so vulnerable. Vance and I think you're being taken advantage of."

"I can tell you one thing. I'm not for one second allowing my relationship with Drake to be put under the Vance-and-Mom microscope."

I took my coffee and went downstairs to get dressed but realized I couldn't bathe unless I hauled in buckets of rain and dumped them in the tub. After bringing in several pailfuls, I splashed soap and water on my body. I propped up a mirror on the windowsill by the bed, sat down on the floor, and started to braid my unwashed hair. I hated the sight of my pink and misty eyes, for anytime I determined to stand strong against Mom, tears betrayed my fear. I felt like a child again, one far too easily thrown into emotional insecurity by its upset mommy.

Drake came in and sat down on the bed. "What went on up there?"

I gave him a short recap of the conversation.

"Jesus. What makes them think I don't work?" he asked.

"I have no idea."

I went back upstairs in hopes of scoring more coffee. When I came around the corner, Vance stepped in front of me, blocked my way, and put his arms around me. I assumed Mom told him about the kitchen conversation while I'd been downstairs. I rolled my eyes and let him hug me.

I'd mentioned weeks before that I wanted to look at real estate in the area. Drake and I had both grown tired of the extreme Arizona heat. Also, townhome living proved to be quite an adjustment, especially due to residents who dedicated time from their days to catch others' infractions of the subdivision rules and restrictions. Drake had trimmed a tree bordering our driveway due to it dropping rotting olives on his car, and within the hour, the president of the homeowners' association appeared at our front door to investigate. One morning, I didn't bring enough poop bags when I took Oliver for a walk and had to leave a little pile while I went back home, got another bag, then returned to the scene. My neighbor two doors down, who could be seen sitting at his kitchen window for hours a day watching the goings-on among the neighbors, did not know I'd in fact picked up Oliver's poop and reported my egregious behavior at the next HOA meeting.

My desire to look at real estate existed before the storm, before Mom and Vance's intrusion on my relationship with Drake, and prior to the coldness they showed him. But without my permission, Mom had chosen a real estate agent, and she was already on her way to meet with me.

Apparently, my statement about looking at homes *well outside* the area had been ignored, as had other specifics. A house had to be far enough away to make it too difficult for Mom or Vance to drop in whenever they felt like it. Due to noise and other obvious factors, I didn't want to live near schools. The agent—a dead ringer for Martha Stewart—arrived at the house and presented several listings for me to see. All were in the heart of town, close to schools, and near Mom and Vance's house. "You don't want to live far outside of town," Mom said.

"Yes, I do."

"But you do want to be near schools, right?" Martha Stewart asked.

"No. I don't even have children," I said.

We waited at the dining room table while Martha searched for other listings on her computer. As we got up to leave, I moaned inwardly upon seeing that Mom and Vance planned to accompany us. Five of us headed out in the agent's van, in a driving rain so hard that the windshield wipers couldn't even begin to address the downpour. I ended up in the far back seat with Mom, unable to see where Martha drove, and unable to take in any of the surroundings.

At the first home, I immediately turned claustrophobic by trying to move through and around four other people. I didn't bother to go upstairs but instead left through the front door and stood under the eaves, looking at the flower beds. Martha took us to another home, one so narrow and confining, I knew I'd never be able to move my furniture into it. Yet another house she showed us sat off to the side of an unpaved, potholed road. I envisioned being frequently snowed in by storms that left us without food, running water, or electricity.

Martha, apparently exhausted from showing three entirely unsuitable homes, suggested we take a break. The five of us stopped for coffee, then decided to call it a day, ostensibly because of the weather. By now, reports warned that the remnants of Hurricane Frances, although weakened due to traveling over land, were approaching our area for a direct hit.

When the four of us arrived at home, I wanted nothing more

than to collapse on our bed, not talk, and not see anyone's face except Drake's. However, Vance announced that he'd made an appointment with a different real estate agent. Off the four of us went, yet again. We sat around a large conference table while a bored-looking and aloof man asked what I was looking for and how much I wanted to spend. I threw out an approximate price range. "Well, I can tell you, for that price, you're not going to find any property nearby."

"I never wanted property nearby," I said.

"You really do," Mom said.

The agent swiveled in his chair and opened a file cabinet, then sent a brochure sliding across the table to me. "This house has good bones," he said.

"What does that mean?" Mom asked.

"It's been on the market a while. Needs some work, but it's structurally sound."

"Okay, sure," I said, shrugging. "I'll look at it."

I slid the brochure several feet over to Vance, who sat at the head of the table. He shot it back at me without looking.

A short break in the force of the rain allowed me to see the outside of the home. It was a pretty barn-style house with a small pond to the side. Indoors, however, it had popcorn ceilings, smelled of cigars, and even had a pile of dead wasps—an insect of which I am absolutely terrified—in one of the rooms. Still, I could picture the home being a nice place with the right work done to it. We all wandered around for about thirty minutes, then got into the car to head home.

"That house has good bones," Mom said, getting into the front seat.

"That place is a dump," Drake said, sliding in by me.

Later, there was a knock on my bedroom door. Drake was outside peeing in the woods, having decided it was a better option than our waterless toilet that would not flush. I opened the door and found Mom standing in the hallway. "I just wanted to say," she whispered, "Drake has no right to tell you which home you should or shouldn't buy. His opinion doesn't matter."

"I value his opinion."

"That house has good bones," she said.

"Okay."

"Well, I'm telling you, he has no right," she said.

"I like knowing what he thinks," I said.

She rolled her eyes, set her mouth hard, and went back upstairs. Later, the four of us sat at the dining room table, playing gin rummy. Vance didn't speak a word except to call "Gin" when he won a hand. Drake remained pleasant and chatty, ignoring the barbs Mom threw his way. "Mothers see things," she said, looking at him. "Mothers can see things in people others can't."

I considered packing up and getting us a hotel room, but we were now in the midst of a full-blown, dangerous storm. Reports told of homes being washed away, several missing persons, and numerous downed trees and blocked roads. A man came to the front door to tell us the subdivision bridge had collapsed and there was no way in or out by car. Neighbors continued to stop by unannounced to provide updates on damages and plans for repairs. "Are you the daughter who got Vance and your mom back together?" one asked after we were introduced.

"No," I said, trying not to grind my teeth. "That was all Mom's idea."

Drake and I rode out the rest of the visit by making ourselves as scarce as possible, reading together for several hours each day in the den. The day before our scheduled flight back to Arizona, a makeshift bridge was constructed at the subdivision entrance. Mom booked a driver to take Drake and me back to the Atlanta airport, so the four of us went into town for much-needed hot coffee and so Drake and I could pull some cash from an ATM for the trip. "I think I'm going to cancel your driver so Vance and I can take you to the airport," Mom announced that evening.

Please. Just shoot me now. "You two have enough to deal with here. You don't need to spend several hours driving," I said. Vance walked across the room and hugged me.

It was yet another night of disturbed sleep as trees cracked and crashed in the forest around the house. We had to be up at dawn, and the possibility of having set the battery-powered clock incorrectly or sleeping through its alarm weighed on me for hours. The thought of missing our flight and having to reschedule or, god forbid, staying any longer at the house than necessary was unthinkable. When the driver arrived the next morning at six and loaded our bags into the trunk, I gave out stiff hugs, got in the back seat, slammed the car door, and did not wave or look back as we rode away. Crews had worked twenty-four hours a day to remove massive tree trunks from the roads, but I feared that newly downed trees awaited us and might prevent us from leaving the area. Only when we hit the main interstate outside of town did I dare consider dropping my defenses and allowing a physical and emotional crash to come over me. I rested my head against the window and watched the scenery fly by, barely speaking until late that afternoon, when Drake and I stepped into the front door of our home.

Mom called a few days later.

"You're lucky I'm even talking to you," I said.

"Why in the world?" she asked.

"Why? Why? The way you treated Drake, that's why!"

"Well, we were just lookin' out for you. I mean—"

"You were wrong about everything. Everything! Where did you even come up with those wild ideas? You were so rude to him, based on nothing!"

"He didn't like that house you liked. We thought he was gonna try to keep you from movin' up here by us."

"All he did was voice an opinion, Mom."

"Vance and I saw things," she said. "Like when you went to the ATM first. Why did you have to pay for the ride to the airport, not Drake?"

"He and I split the cost, Mom. So what if I used a machine first. You owe him an apology."

"I don't know what you expected from us. I mean, we'd never even met him before. You just sprang him on us out of the blue. We didn't know Drake from Adam."

That was a particularly rich defense, considering the speed at which men became my stepfathers. "I'll tell you something else, Mom. What Drake pays me is my business. Even if I wanted to *pay* a man to live with me and *pay* him to have sex with me, that's my business."

"Well, sometimes situations can be misinterpreted," she said.

"You were wrong."

"Just misinterpreted. Sometimes—"

"Mom. You owe him an apology."

An apology never came. A few months later, I told her of our plans to move to the Austin area.

"Vance and I want to go see the Texas relatives. How about if we coordinate it so he and I meet you and help you look for a house?" Mom asked excitedly.

"Oh, my god. No way. No way am I doing that again. I'll find my own house."

During the silence, I could feel the hurt settle in on her as my comment registered. "Fine!" she said. "If that's the way you want it."

Chapter Twenty-Four

On the morning of my birthday, I came home from working out and found the message light blinking on my answering machine. I pressed Play. "Hi, honey. Daaaaaaaan Hillman here," he said, drawing out his name like a game show announcer. I deleted the message and hung up.

The phone rang a few hours later during lunch. Without thinking, I reached over and answered.

"Hi, honey. It's your dad, Dan."

"Oh. Hi."

"Just calling to wish you a happy birthday."

"Thanks," I said.

"I didn't have your current phone number anymore, so I called Vance, and he gave it to me."

"Oh."

The phone had an extra-long cord that allowed me to wander into the den, away from Drake. Dan lived hundreds of miles away and was only a voice on a telephone line, but as soon as I heard him speak, I felt the power he still held over me.

"Just wanted to call. No matter what anyone says, you're still my daughter."

Still your daughter. "I have to go," I said.

"I love you, honey."

"Bye," I said.

"I love you," he said.

I hung up and dialed Mom and Vance's house in a rage. She

answered the phone. "Dan just called," I said. "He said Vance gave him my number. Why? Why would he do that?"

"How do I reach Dan?" she asked.

I checked the answering machine display and gave her his phone number. She hung up, then called back a few minutes later. "I told him not to call you ever again," she said. "When he asked why, I told him that was a stupid question after what he tried to do to you."

I'd told her at some point in my twenties about Dan getting in bed with me when I was a little girl and putting his hands up my nightgown. Decades had passed, and I was surprised she still remembered. More than anything, I was surprised that she'd chosen to go to bat for me. "What did he say?" I asked.

"He said, 'I don't think I know what you mean.' I told him we don't want anything to do with him and to leave all of us alone."

"Will he do that?" I asked.

"He said, 'Well, you don't have to ask me twice.'"

Vance emailed me immediately and apologized for giving out my number. I was able to piece together Dan having called my grandmother to find me. She wouldn't have had my new number at the townhome but knew Mom and Vance would. My grandmother admitted that Dan called her now and then over the years, and she always gave him any phone numbers he wanted. "I just can't tell that man no, honey," she said.

I could relate. Dan lived hundreds of miles away and was no longer at all a part of our family, yet some of us still allowed him to hold a remnant of sway. It's possible that guilt over the affair led Mom and Vance to keep the door open to occasional contact from him, even decades later. But as far as I know, after the phone call from Mom, he didn't contact anyone in our family ever again.

After my grandmother's death, Mom and I found a copy of the decades-old family portrait taken in the backyard of our Houston turquoise wonderland. Dan, Mom, Debbie, Jimmy, Greyson, and I were all in our places with bright, shining faces. We found the portrait on the floor on its side, between a filing cabinet and a wall in my grandmother's home office. Something or someone had made a long gash through the center of the canvas, damage that would have been nearly impossible to repair. "Do you want this?" Mom asked, picking it up.

"Throw it away," I said.

"You don't want it?"

"No. No one wants any kind of reminder of that."

"You're sure? You really don't want it?"

"Mom. Seriously?"

She shrugged, then removed the canvas from the frame. I carried the portrait outside and tossed it into the dumpster.

My drinking voice cranked up its supportive cheerleading, having been obedient and quiet for what it thought was an unfair amount of time. *You've been sober a long while now. You've learned so much about why you used to drink. It'll be different this time, you'll see. You got this, girl. Cheers!*

Drake and I went out for sushi with one of our friends in the townhome complex. I reached for her sake and took a sip. It hit the back of my mouth and throat with a comforting heat and burning. I flagged down our waiter and asked for a sake of my own. "Are you sure you want to do that?" Drake asked.

"I'm sure."

I blew five years of sobriety and started drinking again every day. I rekindled my relationship with wine—the long-lost and comforting best friend I'd once loved—and for months, she proved that she could still be surprisingly kind and giving. Then a friend from Interlochen called. We hadn't spoken in about thirty years, and our conversation was tremendously entertaining. I believed that wine could only make it more so. I opened a chilled bottle of chardonnay and finished it within about forty-five minutes. Still talking on the phone, and starting to slur my words, I went back to the refrigerator and pulled out a previously opened bottle. And drank it. I looked at the clock and realized I'd consumed almost two bottles of wine in less than two hours.

Either my cell battery died or the call dropped, but I was grateful that the phone conversation abruptly ended. I was smashed. When Drake came home, he found me in bed, complaining about nausea and a racing heart. I blamed it on my new thyroid medication, which I'd started taking that morning. He was so concerned about the state I was in, he tried to contact my doctor, but the office was closed for the day.

I got three hours of sleep, then spent the rest of the night staring at the ceiling. My heart pounded against my chest, and I could swear I smelled alcohol oozing out of my pores through my sweat. I had a doctor's appointment the next morning at nine and dragged myself there, no doubt looking as if I'd been recently exhumed. "What's up with your blood pressure?" my doctor asked. "It's a bit alarming."

I confessed to being sleepless and horrifically hungover. "I'm never having wine again as long as I live."

"That's what they all say," she said, laughing.

But since that day, I have never touched a single drop of wine.

Drake and I found a house we loved in the Texas Hill Country and moved in at the end of 2004. Several months later, we flew to St. Lucia and were married under a gnarl-trunked, massive shrimp tree near the beach. We invited no friends or family.

He wore a Tommy Bahama floral shirt and dark slacks. I wore a simple white cotton dress I'd found online for $100.

We were both barefoot. It started to rain before we took our vows, and the wonderful staff who planned our ceremony were thrilled. "Rain on a wedding day is good luck," they said, beaming at us.

Chapter Twenty-Five

My cell phone rang one morning as I drove down the small
state highway that bordered our house. I checked the display and, seeing it was Mom, pulled off the road. "Hey, Mom.
What's up?"

"I called to tell you . . ." Her voice cracked and she broke into
tears. "Vance died last night."

"Vance is dead?" I said.

"He's dead," Mom said. "He had a heart attack."

Forty years of our lives had included Vance in one way or
another. I had to speak it out loud. "Dead."

"He died in his sleep," she said.

"I'm on the highway. On the way to the doctor. Let me call
you back later, Mom."

"I know you loved him," she said.

I kept it together throughout the appointment and all the way
home, then started aimlessly wandering around outside, pacing
along the line of forest that bordered the back of our house. For
well over an hour, I paced. I'd spoken to him on the phone about
a week before. Drake and I had had to put our schnauzer to sleep.
At sixteen years old, Oliver was blind, deaf, incontinent, and so
arthritic he could no longer stand or walk. When I returned from
the vet appointment, I emailed Mom to tell her. "But please don't
call me to talk about this. It hurts too much."

The day after I'd told her not to contact me, Vance called.
He'd recently been diagnosed with dementia after a year or so of

varying diagnoses from different doctors. It progressed quickly, taking away his ability to drive, handle his own medications, or read. Soon, he could only answer yes or no questions and could no longer form sentences, so I was surprised to receive a phone call from him. "I just called . . . ," he said.

"To say I'm sorry," Mom whispered in the background.

"To say I'm sorry," he said.

"About Oliver's death . . . ," Mom whispered.

"About Oliver's death," he said.

"I can't talk about this," I said brusquely, and hung up.

Mom denied she'd had anything to do with the call. I couldn't forget having been so harsh with Vance in our last conversation. I continued to wander around outside and review the stress-filled and convoluted history that made up my relationship with him. I rued the number of times I'd wanted him to simply vanish somehow; I'd always envisioned a life without him as less complicated and far less confusing. I'd gotten my wish.

Mom called me with ideas for funerals. Plural of funeral. "Why not just have one?" I asked.

She wanted to have a ceremony in their state of residence and another in Texas. It had always surprised me that Vance wanted to be buried in the Texas cemetery where most of *our* family members are instead of with *his* family. I'd never asked him why, as he might view the questions as hostile or strangely territorial. "Mom, you're making everyone go all the way to the East Coast too?" I said. "Why not have the Texas funeral for all of our family that lives in Texas and another for all your friends on the East Coast?"

"Well, that's a great idea, but that's not what I'm going to do," she said. "We're going to have two funerals."

Frankly, this sounded like one big royal pain in the ass and, yes, a huge personal inconvenience. Mom had determined when Greyson and I would fly in, also how many days we'd be there, and she wanted to make our flight reservations for us. We were to stay with her, of course, but she planned to allow her daughter-in-law, son-in-law, and their two children to stay at the house as well. Like my visit during my ballet performance, and when Jane went to Connecticut with me during Mom's divorce, sharing a room with Mom meant I could look forward to about four hours of interrupted sleep every night. Warning signals flashed. *Control! Manipulation! Sleep deprivation!*

Over coffee in bed the next morning, I told Drake of the multiple funeral plans and Mom's tightening tendrils regarding how and for how long I had to participate. "Mom, Mom, Mom. Always Mom," I said, my voice rising.

"Wow. You really need to get over this thing with your mother," Drake said.

"Fuck her!" I yelled.

"Maybe like some professional—"

"Get over this thing? You don't get it! It's not like she did something to me fifty years ago and I can't move on. No, that really might be pathetic. There's no part of my life where Mom isn't inserted somehow, and—"

"Okay," he said. "But for your own sake . . ."

After Drake left for work that morning, I did an online search for a therapist and found one that specialized in family relations. There wasn't much else to go on, but the photo on his website portrayed a nice face and gentle smile. He looked like a man with whom it would be easy to spill my guts. Or spew my guts, for Vance's death had brought up a roiling ball of confusion, remorse, guilt, anger, and resentment. I resented feeling like a powerless child who had no say whatsoever about her mother's intrusions. I wanted to scream at her to do whatever she wanted with her life but, from that day forward, to make decisions that didn't always affect me.

I left a message on the therapist's voicemail. He returned my call within the hour. "What issue led you to me?" he asked.

I started to cry. "I really don't think my mother loves me."

I culled through literally thousands of slides Mom had given me of our family, many dating back to Greyson and me in infancy and extending up to her marriage to Vance. I threw away all slides that included him, preferring to keep a few print photographs instead. Coincidentally, Vance's daughter emailed me to say she had photos of her mother and Mom. I knew all had been taken when the two women were friends, before the affair was discovered. His daughter asked if I would be interested in having the originals and provided a montage of several, complete with her commentary on each. She wrote:

"Here's a photo of your mom with my mother. My mother was a very loyal person and trusted her friends."

"Here's another, taken before the two couples went to dinner together one evening. Your mother put false eyelashes on my mom. Although your mother wore false eyelashes all the time, mine was naturally beautiful and did not need them."

"This is a nice picture of them as well. Two women who were supposedly close friends. Never in her wildest dreams would my mother suspect she'd be betrayed."

I emailed back:

"I'm up to my neck in my own project now, going through hundreds of slides. The last thing I need is more photos. Thanks so much for thinking of me, though!"

Sick of the constant mama-drama, I started a blog as a creative means of venting my anger and frustration. I called it *My Mother Committed Serial Marriage*. The first post was titled "Life with

Mom," the graphics for which were a GIF of subatomic parti-
cles represented by multicolored swirling arcs and flashing lights,
all moving in a revolving, constant pattern around one another.
The corresponding text presented the story of how Mom and
Dad divorced at the same time Dan and Patsy divorced, resulting in the two couples switching partners with one another and
marrying.

My brother-in-law was one of the first to follow the blog.
"Isn't this going to offend your mother?" he wrote.

"My mother sees, hears, and processes nothing regarding the
divorces," I replied. As I saw it, she had so emotionally compart-
mentalized the effects of her actions, the existence of the blog
could only naturally remain outside her awareness as well. Also,
working her way around the internet was a bit challenging for
her, and it wasn't as if my blog had gone viral. I posted about once
a week, then maybe once a month, and soon all but forgot about
its existence.

I noted that my therapist was amazingly tall, just like my biological father. Same ice-blue eyes. "You don't make good decisions
when you drink," he said. "There's a lot of work to be done here,
and I want you to do it without alcohol."

I nodded. I'd confessed to having six beers a day but considered any amount over that to be "excessive." Like many drinkers,
I'd attempted to switch over to beer, believing it's difficult to
drink many glasses of it. Beer did have a way of keeping my
drinking behavior more in line. If I drank in "excess," most of
the night would be spent lying awake and staring at the ceiling.
Also, if I drank too far beyond the level of tipsy, I risked Drake
discovering my secret. Managing the daily accumulation of beer
cans added to the stress. I tossed all of them under the laundry room sink, a place Drake had no reason to explore. When

the accumulated number grew alarming, I smashed them, threw them into a Hefty garbage bag, and drove them to the aluminum can drop-off site several miles down the highway.

I agreed to stop drinking. Unbeknownst to my therapist, I didn't plan to do so until my alcohol stash was, shall we say, liquidated. How wasteful to dispose of perfectly good liquor without first allowing its loveliness to pass through me! That afternoon and the next, I polished off the rest of my alcohol. Then I stopped. When I returned to the next session, I reported that I had trouble sleeping but surprisingly was not white-knuckling it without drinking, even though I'd remained fully riled all week about Vance's upcoming funerals.

"So, how about just not going?" my therapist asked.

It never failed to surprise me over the years when people assumed standing up to Mom was a simple act. The potential blowback from her had always reined me in, and it seemed inconceivable that others could be so nonchalant when making similar decisions involving their mothers. What would people think of me? I could already see all heads shaking in disapproval. *What could possibly be more important at this time than helping to see her mother through her grief? She's lost her husband, after all!* "Not go? That would be unthinkable! What would it look like if I didn't go to my own stepfather's funeral?" I said.

"Why do you care so much about what people think?" he asked.

"Christ, this is complicated! Why does everything involving Mom have to be so complicated?"

"You tell me why it's so complicated, Sondra. You told me when you first contacted me that you don't believe your mother loves you. Tell me why."

I continued relating memories. Memories I'd recounted so many times to so many therapists. Story after story of my mother's actions that made me feel unnecessary and pushed aside, a recounting of history that seemed to lead nowhere, a retelling that had never led to deep understanding or healing. "But she did so much for me. She spent years of my childhood driving me everywhere. Hours and hours a week. Making my costumes. Accompanying me on the piano. But almost everywhere she took me, she left me."

"What do you mean, left you?" he asked.

"I'd wait for her for hours at times. In the heat, in the dark, or on a downtown street corner. I couldn't get mad. I wasn't allowed to get mad. She did so much for me. How can I forget all she did for me?"

He stared out the window behind me, deep in thought for a few moments. "What did you say your dog's name was, Sondra? The one you recently lost?"

"Oliver," I said.

"Okay. So, what if you had told Oliver's groomer, 'When you finish with him, just put him out on the sidewalk. I'll get there when I get there.'" He waved his hand in the air, as if throwing trash over his shoulder.

I pictured Oliver alone and confused, not knowing how to find me. He'd pace about, searching the faces of passing people with those alert, humanlike eyes of his, wanting me to be there, not understanding why I was not. "I would never do that to him! He'd be so scared!"

My therapist gave me time to process this. He shifted in his chair, always adjusting his long, long legs. "What's your mother's story? Her childhood story. You can bet she has one."

"She doesn't bring it up much. She did say her father abandoned them when she was a young girl. Her mother had to work and wasn't available to her, at least not like other mothers back then."

"And how old is she now?"

"Early seventies."

"It's sad," he said. "It's doubtful she'll ever have a truly connected, heart relationship. Time may have run out for her to ever find that."

I walked into my therapist's office for my next appointment, stopped, and looked around. "Did you rearrange your furniture?" I asked.

"No, and would you believe you're the third person this week to ask me that?"

I took my usual place on the couch that backed up to the windows that looked out onto the parking lot. Before each session, I provided a status on my drinking without being asked. "No, I didn't drink this week."

"How does it feel?"

"I'm really bummed. One of our cats is missing. I've been searching all over the neighborhood looking for her."

"Oh, I'm sorry," he said.

"I lost three pounds from walking," I said.

"Wow."

I sighed and met his gaze with a "where do we start?" expression.

"I'm sorry about your cat."

I nodded.

Silence. He waited. His eyebrows were up. There was the tilt of his head that was growing familiar. "Did something else happen?"

I looked down at my hands, then pulled tissue from the box on the end table to my right. "There's so much Kleenex in this room," I said, looking around at all the boxes. He nodded. "Sometimes it scares me. The level of anger I feel toward her." Another head tilt from him. "Sometimes I think I hate her. Not always, but . . ." I wished he would finish more of my sentences for me. He settled back in his chair and placed the ankle of one of his legs upon the opposite knee. "There's something I can't get my mind around. Something I can't work out."

"Let's talk about it then," he said.

"Okay," I said, steeling myself. A car alarm went off in the parking lot behind me. It was not the first time it had happened during one of our sessions, but he and I had learned to work around it. The owner of the car never came out to turn it off. I shrugged, then began. "I'd have to be about seven or eight, I guess. I remember our babysitter, Mrs. Hugly, making me stay in bed, so I must have been sick. She always included grapes with my lunches. I hated grapes. I threw all of them between my bed and the wall."

"Sounds like something my daughter would do," my therapist said with a small smile.

"Mrs. Hugly was with me for a few days, so Mom and Dan were obviously out of town. But then we're suddenly in the new house. I specifically remember Dan calling out from the top of the stairs, telling me to come up to the master bedroom. When I enter the doorway, I find him lying on his stomach on the bed."

"Take off your clothes," Dan says. "We have to make sure you're over the mumps."

I paused, still trying to piece together the sequence of images. Mrs. Hugly must have been nursing me through the mumps—or maybe chicken pox. I couldn't remember.

Dan orders me to take off my clothes. I reach around to the back of my neck and undo the single large button of my one-piece culotte paja-mas. I let them drop to the floor. I still have my underwear on. Dan waits. I slide them down and step out when they drop to the carpet. "Get on the bed and lie down," Dan says.

I crawl onto the bed and stretch out on my back. I'm only a few feet away from him. In my peripheral vision, I can see the slow movement of his head as his eyes travel the full length of my body. As he studies every inch of me, I stare at the white ceiling. Frozen. All around me, I'm surrounded by endless hot pink. Dan pushes himself forward on his forearms. His face is now only inches from my crotch. So close, I can feel his breath on my thigh.

The memory so disgusted me, I had to stop speaking.

"Go on . . . ," my therapist said a while later, almost in a whisper.

I shook my head and stared at my lap. I'd wadded tissues around three of the fingers on my left hand. I'd repeatedly mutilated the cuticles the prior week, leaving bloody and ragged skin. I adjusted the Kleenex to hide the disgusting mess from my therapist. "Dan's face is only inches away," I said. "His fingers probe me, explore me, as if to see what a little girl looks like down there."

I stared off into the corner, off to the side of my therapist. He shifted in his chair and leaned slightly, as if trying to get in my line of sight. "Tell me what else, Sondra. Tell me."

I burst into tears. I was twisting the tissue around and around my fingers; my efforts were wadding it up. I had to stop if I was going to hide the mutilation. I balled my hands into fists. "My mother was there!" I blurted out.

My therapist looked stricken. "Oh, no. No," he said.

"My mother was on the bed! Stretched out on her side, all relaxed. Like she was just lying there watching television. She did nothing! Nothing to protect me. Nothing to stop him!" I was trembling. "It was always the timing I couldn't figure out until now. But the hot pink. Everything was hot pink."

"What was hot pink?" he asked. "Tell me."

"Their bedroom! And my being out of school for a week—that was first grade. That means she saw his abuse early on!"

"Sondra, I'm so sorry."

"What kind of mother lets a man inspect her daughter's body that way?" I yelled. I was sobbing now, and my therapist was letting me cry it out. After a few minutes, I was almost quiet again.

"What are you feeling now?" he asked. "Tell me what you're feeling physically, Sondra."

"My heart's pounding. I'm shaky. I'm so cold!" I said, rubbing my arms.

"In a very real way, you just relived the experience. Our bodies don't always know the difference."

I took a deep breath and tried to slow my heartbeat.

"He showed her what he was early on, Sondra. She knew. The danger was clear."

The following week, I plopped down on the couch. "No, I didn't drink. And something else happened." I wanted a drumroll. All I got was a tilt of his head.

"Okay . . ."

"Right before I left to come here, I sent an email to her. I told her I'll go to the Texas funeral but not the East Coast one."

"What did she say?" he asked.

"Don't know yet. I got in the car and came here. I was scared to press send, but I did it."

When I returned home, I found she'd already replied. She wrote: "I'm really disappointed. You could have been a help to me in so many ways." I felt no guilt. My attendance at one funeral would have to suffice.

Although I'd unearthed my mother's greatest betrayal of my trust, never once did I consider discussing it with her. I could never in a million years bring myself to detail what she allowed Dan's fingers to do to me that day. I knew with all certainty that had I brought it up to her, she would claim no memory of it or would insist that the abuse did not happen, then assure me she would never have allowed such a violation of my body. The discovery of her betrayal that day on the bed set in motion the process of separating my identity from hers. I finally knew I was not an extension of her. So confident was I in the strength and validity of my metamorphosis, I didn't return to therapy after that day, believing the discovery of my separateness had more than satisfied my reasons for seeking professional help.

I'd kept my promise to my therapist and had remained alcohol-free during the several weeks we'd worked together. My drinking brain viewed this as cause for celebration, and I did not disappoint. I was soon back up to pre-therapy level of a six-pack a day.

Chapter Twenty-Six

Late one afternoon in September 2011, Drake and I had just settled in to watch a movie when we saw a large cloud of dust, caused by someone driving at an alarmingly high speed up our driveway. I went to the master bathroom and opened the window that looked out on our front gate. A young man jumped out of his truck and came running toward the house. "What is it?" I called out.

He searched for where the voice had come from and saw me in the window. "Ma'am, there's a wildfire comin' this way, and you better get out quick!"

I looked toward the forest that bordered the rear of our property and saw huge black waves of smoke rolling toward us. "Jesus Christ!" I yelled and slammed the window.

Drake and I had smelled smoke earlier in the day but figured it was a nearby barbecue grill or maybe neighbors burning brush. Soon, the power went out. No power, no water, and no television to track the progress of the fire. A friend in Austin called me with frequent updates about our area. The fires continued to jump back and forth over the nearby highway, and our home was only several hundred feet from the road. A sheriff's car came up the driveway, and we met the officer out by the gate. "If that fire jumps the highway again, you're right in its path. This is a mandatory evacuation. Get your things together and leave," she said.

A friend let us stay with her. The next morning, I drove into town to PetSmart to buy dog food. When I came back to the car, I saw Mom's number on my cell phone display and was touched that she'd thought to check on our safety. I returned her call. She picked up and started a breezy chat. "Mom. Stop," I said. "We were evacuated from the house."

"Why?" she asked. Although the fires were constant national news, she said she had not known of them. She told me about a new man she'd recently met at her church. "He's a retired dentist," she said. "He showed up unannounced the other morning and flossed my teeth."

The tree-filled land behind us was entirely scorched and looked like a bombed-out war zone. Our house was spared, and we were allowed to return home. Small fires continued to erupt throughout the area, and helicopters flew over night and day to drop water. Our home no longer felt safe to me, making sleep nearly impossible. I lived out of a suitcase for days on end in case we were ordered to leave at a moment's notice. The sound of any helicopter overhead threw me into a panic, and I was afraid to leave the house for even the smallest errand, for fear a new fire would prevent my return.

I called Mom, wanting to wrest a shred of concern from her. "It never ends. Days and days and days—"

"He's on his way over. I really can't talk," she said.

"I'm so afraid. Fires keep popping up in the area. I can't even sleep."

"He'll be here any minute. I'm making him a hamburger."

"I think I'm having panic attacks," I said, my voice growing more and more desperate.

"I really can't talk now."

"I can't calm—"

"He just drove up," she said excitedly. "I have to go."

She called a few weeks later. "I wanted to tell you, I had a stroke," she said.

"A stroke? Oh my god! Are you okay?"

"I really didn't even feel anything when it happened," she said. "But part of my hand went numb, and I was draggin' my foot."

"What did they say at the hospital? What about that drug they give, the one that has to be given within an hour—"

"I didn't go to the hospital."

"What?"

"I said I didn't go."

"You had a stroke and didn't even go to the emergency room?"

"I'm happier than I've ever been in my life, and I wasn't gonna do anything to mess it up," she said.

The image she proceeded to present of her new, retired-dentist boyfriend was of a man who might grow bored and fidgety during her hospital stay, then drift toward the company of another woman. I decided then and there I did not like him.

They married shortly thereafter. I made a game of seeing how long I could go without meeting husband number seven and made it to almost one year.

Mom and I sat in the living room of the Louisiana house where she and her husband, Dave, spent several months of the year. It was a historical home, although maybe not officially registered as such, and used to be some sort of chop house at the turn of the century. There was a framed copy of an old menu hanging on the wall in the kitchen. The front door was so close to the street, it was easy to imagine the horse-drawn carriages arriving and depositing diners directly onto the front steps.

Mom had strung up plastic Christmas candles on the windowsills, which normally would have struck me as rather cheesy, but the effect from outside looked especially beautiful through the sleety rain we'd endured for days. Their home looked warm and welcoming from the street.

During my visit to their other home several months before,

Mom had mentioned around four o'clock one afternoon that a glass of wine sure sounded nice. "No alcohol before five! There will be no alcoholics in this house!" Dave had bellowed.

But drinking rules are made to be broken; I knew this as well as anyone. Somewhere between my two visits, Dave had relaxed his edict regarding the acceptable time of day for a supposed non-alcoholic to start drinking, and they started off with sherry around three in the afternoon. I still drank only beer, but Dave had gone on and on about making the best martinis in the world. I threw caution to the wind. "Prove it," I said.

The drink he placed on the end table by me was not as bitter as I'd expected. I only allowed myself hard liquor once a year— one martini on New Year's Eve—and the holidays were still weeks away. His martini was nowhere close to the best I'd ever had, but I didn't let on. The three of us chatted while we drank, then he excused himself to get dressed for a housewarming party being held down the street.

I went to the guest room to retrieve a DVD I'd made as a surprise for Mom. It consisted of old slides of her, Greyson, and me from the sixties and seventies, the images of which had been turned into a professional montage with a soundtrack. I came back into the den and handed the disk to her. "I have a surprise for you," I said.

She turned it over and over in her hand, studying it. "Is this from the slides I gave you a while back?"

"You'll just have to see. I had it made especially for you."

"Will this embarrass me?" she asked.

"Who knows?"

"Don't make me have to kill you," she said.

The two of us went into the master bedroom, the only room in the house with a television. She walked to the console at the far wall and adeptly worked the remote to turn on the television and disc player. Her competence with technology surprised me.

She stretched out on the bed, not looking at all enthusiastic. I took the chair off to her side, in the corner.

She pressed PLAY. A series of photos started to roll, about one every five seconds. There Greyson and I were as babies, propped up with pillows on the couch in officers' housing in Maryland. Early sixties. Such big smiles! Mom had once told me she used to watch *The Secret Storm* on that ugly blue couch every afternoon while she fed us.

Dave breezed through the master bedroom, barely giving the video a glance. "Honey, stay and watch this with us," Mom said.

He stopped and looked at the screen, right when a photo of my dad in his Navy uniform appeared, walking past a line of bombers on an airfield. "That's my father," I told Dave, who nodded and feigned interest. I wondered if Mom felt uncomfortable with him seeing a photo of Dad. She'd once intimated that Dave wasn't much interested in her past. He seemed to have the attention span of a gnat this afternoon and continued on to somewhere else in the house.

Look at Dad in that uniform. Handsome . . . oh my god.

There I am, singing in the living room. It's turquoise, so that had to be the 1970s. There are a few Dan years left.

Lulu with Mom. God, that dog adored her. Vance was so jealous of all the affection Lulu got, he said Mom had an abnormal attraction to her. To a dog!

Me, onstage. There I am, getting a trophy for singing "Cabaret" in a talent show.

Dave walked past again as another photo of me appeared, singing in the living room of the turquoise wonderland. My wide-open mouth revealed a large gap between my front teeth and countless silver fillings in the molars. I thought for sure he'd comment on them, being a retired dentist.

"Why'd you stop singing? You should be singing. Looks like you enjoyed it," he said.

"I did a lot of it because I was, I guess, expected to," I said, sneaking a glance at Mom. "Sorry, Mom," I added, not meaning to infer that she'd forced me. She didn't acknowledge my comment and still hadn't said a single word about the photos.

Greyson, slightly chubby in his preteen years, looking at the camera with a pained expression. Dan always demanded smiles for photos. Greyson managed one as best he could. Dan made him such an outsider all those years.

The deep-sea fishing trip in Mazatlán, so many summers ago! Mom got food poisoning at a cheap diner. I doubt she remembers. That dead striped marlin on the back of the boat was mine. There's Greyson, sitting in a swivel deck chair. So much activity around him while he reads a book, ignored.

I sneaked a peek at Mom. Her expression was intense, her brow furrowed. Dave was walking through the bedroom again, this time on his way to the kitchen, when a photo of Mom appeared. She was on a beach, wearing an oversized orange sun hat that looked like a terra-cotta pot. No makeup, and with white zinc stuff dabbed above her upper lip. She'd always feared getting brown sunspots. "Mom liked to wear upside-down flowerpots on her head," I joked to Dave. He offered a small smile on his way to the master bathroom.

The next photo was a duplicate of her in the flower-pot hat. "Honey, come watch! I want you to see this with us," Mom said. He stopped at the end of the bed, folded his arms, and produced a small, wooden smile. After less than a minute, he turned fidgety again, most likely grateful to be due soon at the party down the street.

There's Mom in the kitchen at the Memorial Drive apartment. She was married to Vance then, but I hadn't included a single photo of him.

That dress! The floor-length black one with the little flowers on it. She could still fit into it if she still had it. She's in full makeup with false eyelashes. How did she possibly go through that beauty regimen every morning? Teased, puffy hair. Always sprayed with Aqua Net.

"Mom, I think that's the most beautiful photo of you ever taken," I said. She seemed to consider the possibility.

Such a tired and sad-looking man, seated at the table, surrounded by a wall of turquoise, with a cup of black coffee and a half-empty pack of filterless Camel cigarettes in front of him.

"Who's that?" Mom asked.

"That's your dad," I said, looking over at her. She looked confused. He'd spent days on end sitting at that table smoking. What else could he do? It wasn't as if he ever wanted to be part of Mom's life. I remember him giving me a five-dollar bill. It seemed like all the money in the world to a nine-year-old. She and I would see him only once more before he died in 1974.

Mom, asleep, in that huge hot-pink bed. Our Pomeranian, Lulu, is so cute, sleeping with her, right by her head. The morning sun comes through the sheer curtains.

"You look like an angel, Mom," I said.

Mom again, seated at the candlelit marble dinner table. She always set a beautiful table. Still does. Steak and salad on her plate. Her wine glass is half empty. She looks a bit sad. Resigned, even. What was she thinking? Was she having the affair with Vance yet?

The camera effect slow-dissolved, closing in around her face as the music faded. She was so, so beautiful.

I looked over at her on the bed. She was lost in thought and hadn't smiled. Maybe I'd thrown too many memories at her. I'd never gotten a good feel for how much introspection she allowed herself. The television screen went dark. Mom clicked STOP on the remote and got up from the bed. "Let's go back to the den," she said.

There was still some martini left in my glass. I took another large swig of it. "You need to go easy on that," Mom said.

Dave returned to the den and sat with us, and they started in on a glass of wine. "Gotta catch up with you two," I said, downing the rest of my drink.

"You want another one?" Dave asked.

"Sure!" I said.

Mom frowned, watching him disappear into the kitchen. He returned and handed me the glass. I took a sip. "What did you put in this?" I asked. "What's your special recipe?"

"I didn't mix up anything special," he said. "I've been giving you straight vodka."

Straight vodka doth not a martini make. I didn't even like vodka, but it went down more and more easily as the sips went by. *Well, in for a penny, in for a pound.* Dave excused himself and went into the bedroom to watch sports. He still hadn't left for the party but always made a habit of being showered, dressed, and ready for an event long before it began.

I was surprised at how little of Mom there was in the den—in the entire house, really—the only distinctive Mom touch being her miniature Christmas tree, which sat on top of an antique piece of furniture that must have belonged to Dave. It was his house, after all, but Mom usually added her own style to a new place. Not here. The ornaments on the fake little tree were tiny, ornate shoes, which I recognized from a Neiman Marcus collection. I'd given her two of the designs a few Christmases ago.

A book I'd given them, *Underwater Dogs*—photos taken of dogs diving, swimming, or reveling in water—rested on the coffee table. "Alma would have loved this book," I said, picking it up and thumbing through it. There wasn't a thing in the world my grandmother wouldn't have done for a dog. There were times when she had as many as five strays, and Mom and I both had inherited her love for animals.

"Yeah, she would have," Mom said.

"Was it odd having a working mother back in the forties?"

She looked as if she had to think about it for a second. "She sure wasn't like other mothers, but I was really proud of her," Mom said.

"But I mean, weren't your feelings hurt that she couldn't participate much in your life when you were growing up?"

"I didn't realize this was gonna turn into a therapy session," Mom said. I waited as she shifted her weight and readjusted her bare foot, which for as long as I could remember, she made the habit of tucking under herself anytime she relaxed on a chair or couch. I'd picked up the habit from her. "Well, I had to get myself to and from all my music lessons and rehearsals. All my friends' mothers took 'em and picked 'em up. And on school days, Lu and I had to get ourselves home and back to school from lunch. No one would pick us up or take us back."

"I can't believe no one ever thought to do that," I said.

"It was really stressful," she added. "And no one ever made dinner. My grandmother would make breakfast and lunch, but we were on our own the rest of the time."

"Why in the world wouldn't she cook dinner for you?" I asked.

"I don't know. I think she thought she was gettin' too fat. She had a normal-looking body but this huge stomach. It may have been a tumor." I'd seen my great-grandmother's death certificate on Ancestry.com. She'd died of diabetes.

"Honey, you coming with me?" Dave asked, breezing through the room.

"No, you go. I'm gonna sit here and talk to my daughter," Mom said. We watched him fiddling around and buzzing about in the kitchen for a minute or so. Unless there was a sports event on television or a drink in his hand, the guy just couldn't sit still. Finally, we heard the kitchen door shut.

"But I remember lookin' out my bedroom window sometimes, really late at night, and I'd see Mother down there in her office. It was so late, and she'd have the light on over her drafting table. My father was away in the Army, and she had so much to do to try and keep us afloat financially. She was always workin'."

I stole a glance at my drink. I'd almost finished my second "martini" and considered getting up and pouring another. "God, Cissie," Mom said, looking at my glass.

"You were beautiful and so musically talented," I said. "I never understood why you didn't go with that. Go to Hollywood. Become a musician . . . I don't know."

"Bein' from such a small town, we just never thought that way," she said. She looked wistful and sad. "I really could've had a lot of power," she said.

"I could have too," I said.

"Yeah, you really could have," she said. "So, anyway, I met your father. I didn't want to live at home anymore, so I said I'd marry him. He really wasn't a good husband or father, sorry to say."

"No, it's okay. I know he wasn't. I remember Patsy saying one of his girlfriends used to send letters to the house. She'd write things like, 'I always think of you when I wash my hair.'" Mom rolled her eyes. "I asked Patsy why she stayed with Dad. She said she had kids to feed."

For so many years, I'd thought less of Patsy for staying with such a womanizer, even though that womanizer was my father. It hadn't registered yet that women of that generation had so few options regarding credit, jobs, and even the ability to buy a car on their own.

"I did pack you and Greyson up and drive all the way from Maryland to Texas. I was so disgusted with your dad, I was gonna leave him. But I decided to go back."

"What made you?" I asked.

"For one thing, Susie was about to have puppies," Mom said. Susie was our long-gone beagle, and her adoption may have even predated Greyson's and my birth. I understood Mom's decision to return because of a pregnant dog. I would have done the same, even if it meant returning to a dead marriage. "But then when he got out of the service and we came home from the party that night, he admitted he'd been seein' someone. From that second on, I didn't give a whit about him," she said, waving her arm in the air as if brushing him aside. "I couldn't have cared less," she said.

"And then you met Dan," I said.

"I was glad Dan came along when he did. I didn't know how I was gonna take care of you two."

"Dan said he went to see your attorney with you, and you said you didn't want custody of us, that Dad could have us. Dan said he convinced you to keep us."

She didn't answer. The features of my face hardened as a familiar heat rose in my brain. I knew all too well the warning signs of hard alcohol cueing pent-up aggression to stand up and demand to be heard. Years before, I'd sworn to stop drinking tequila after I got in a two-hour argument with Kyle, all the while not knowing what we were fighting about and unsure of what winning looked like, considering how far off topic we'd veered. About thirty minutes into my fight with him, I no longer knew why I was angry. I'd never touched tequila again.

Vodka, meet Sondra. Sondra . . . vodka.

"While I was watchin' the DVD you brought, I felt sick to my stomach. All those sweet pictures of Greyson, and the reminder of what Dan did to him. I just wanted to scream seein' him as that sweet little boy. I felt sick, literally sick to my stomach."

I looked at my glass. It was empty—forlornly so—and thunderously calling out to me for rescue. "And yet you did nothing, Mom."

"But I didn't know! I didn't know at the time what Dan was doing."

"The fuck you didn't! Three or four times a week Greyson

got the belt, and you didn't know? I used to hide on the floor between my bed and the wall so I wouldn't hear him screaming!"

Mom shook her head back and forth.

"I could hear him screaming all the way at the other end of the house, Mom!"

"I didn't know!" she said.

"Well, you fucking should have known. Don't you remember his little red eyes at dinner and his face all puffy from crying?"

She angled her body away from me and shook her head harder.

"God damn it!" I yelled. "I am so fucking mad at you!"

"Honey, I've always known you were mad at me." She stated this with such nonchalance, she may as well have said she'd always known I liked broccoli.

"And when Patsy pulled a gun on me, did you even call the police?"

"I knew she wasn't gonna shoot you."

"You *knew* she wasn't going to shoot me? Someone has a gun pointed at your daughter's head, but you just *know* they're not going to pull the trigger? Just how the hell did you know that, Mom?"

"I wasn't thinkin' right. I really wasn't. I wanted to divorce Dan, and—"

"And when I came running into the house, you let him take a belt to me. Because I didn't come when you called. Why would you let him do that, Mom? Dan's yelling at me to come inside, but there's a gun pointed at my face!"

Never had I spewed such venom at her. And yet, she for some reason remained in her chair. It wasn't as if I wanted her to come out swinging, but her excessive calm was infuriating. "What can I do?" she asked. "What can I do? You can't even tell me you love me. I tell you I love you all the time in my emails, but you can't do it. I see it. I know it. You just can't tell me you love me." No,

I couldn't. "I asked Dave the other night to tell me he loved me, but he wouldn't do it. I just about lost it with him," she said.

I burst into tears. "I do love you, Mom. But you're not safe! I can't trust you with my feelings."

"What can I do?" she asked.

"You never protected Greyson or me!" I said, my voice rising. "I want to hear you say, just for once, 'I totally fucked things up and I'm sorry'!"

She got up from her chair, came over, and stood in front of me. She bent down, gently took my face in her hands, and looked me square in the eyes. "Honey, I totally fucked things up, and I'm sorry." I had to look away.

Dave walked in the door, ending our conversation. She went back to her chair and sat down. For the rest of the evening, she couldn't keep from touching my face or reaching out to stroke my hair. She even tucked me into bed that night. She pulled the covers up around me and placed her palm on my forehead. "My sweet little daughter," she said.

Several months later, Drake headed off to the airport for his annual summer trip to see family and celebrate his mother's birthday. He planned to be gone for over a week, leaving me in a silent home with no need to cook, clean, or adhere to any kind of schedule. Bliss.

I had just stepped out of the shower when the phone rang. Normally, I'd have ignored the call and dealt with it later but wondered if Drake might have a problem with his flight. My phone was in the kitchen, so I carefully made my way across the stained concrete floors, hoping my feet were dry enough to prevent slipping. I caught the phone on the last ring. It was Mom. "Uh, hey," she said, tentatively. "I just got a call from the rattlesnake."

The rattlesnake was one of Dave's daughters. Mom had

reached the point where she didn't even relay the message if the rattlesnake called the house wanting to talk to her father. Mom had justified this to me by saying she was not a secretary. "The rattlesnake and I got into an email tiff," Mom said. "I told her I was sick and tired of her hostile attitude. She wrote me back and said, 'Always pretending to be such a Christian, aren't you? Playing organ for church and all. I guess what your daughter writes about you in her blog is true.'"

I slapped my hand over my mouth. *Oh, god. Oh god, no. No, no, no, please. No.*

"What does she mean about a blog?" Mom asked.

Nothing nothing nothing, no. Think, think, think. "There's a blog, Mom. I had a blog called *My Mother Committed Serial Marriage.*" *Christ. Why did I tell her what it was called? Shut up shut up shut up.* "It was a while ago. I never even—"

"What are we gonna do about this?" Mom asked.

"Let me think for a minute. I'll call you back." *How could you have been so stupid? Stupid stupid stupid stupid.* I went back to the bathroom and turned on the shower. As soon as I stepped under the water, I realized I'd already taken a shower. I stepped out and dried off again.

The phone rang. It was Mom. "Have you figured out what to do about this?" she asked.

"No. I need some time. Just let me—"

"Call me," she said, and hung up.

I dialed Drake's cell number. The blaring sound of an intercom in the background told me he hadn't yet left the airport. "Mom called. The rattlesnake told her about the blog. I think I'm gonna be sick."

"Oh, weeeeellll," he said. "Nothing to be done about it now, I guess."

I paced back and forth in our kitchen. "What do I do? Oh, Christ. I'm starting to panic!"

"Is it really that big of a deal? So you wrote a few blog posts about her."

"She's not going to drop this. She's already called twice. She expects me to do something."

"It's done, baby. You started a blog, you wrote about her, she found out."

"This is gonna be bad. God, I wish you were here," I said.

"I have to go. They're calling my flight."

"Call me back soon. Okay? Promise?"

I called Greyson to warn him. Mom would call in reinforcements on this one. She habitually recruited as many family members and friends as possible to support her side against a perceived aggressor. This time, that aggressor was me, and a mammoth emotional conflagration was a certainty. "You have to get over this thing you have against Mom!" Greyson said.

"But you don't understand. The blog was a few years ago. I'd forgotten all about it."

"Well, it's just gonna take time for her to get over this. Not much you can do about it now."

Mom's calls started coming in again, but I didn't pick up. The number of messages grew, but I didn't call back.

Greyson called the next day. "You have to call her. She's devastated. I've never seen her so hurt. She said the one person she believed would never do such a thing to her has done it."

"I didn't do this on purpose, I swear."

"Call her. Tell her you didn't intentionally try to hurt her."

"I don't want to call her," I said.

"Call her. I feel like I'm standing here watching my family fall apart."

And still, I didn't call. But I packed up all my beer in a garbage bag, drove to a small country gas station a few miles away, and tossed it all into a trash can. For the next few days, I couldn't eat, and I barely slept. Normally, I allowed myself to find solace in alcohol. I vowed to face this problem without it.

Three days later, I called her. I stood in the kitchen with the phone held away from my ear. I had never heard Mom shriek, not at anyone or anything. "What kind of daughter does such a thing?" she wailed. I put the phone close to my ear again, ready to deliver my defensive reply, but then the shrieking started. "What kind? I've tried to make a life here. Now everyone in town is going to know about this!"

"Mom, not everyone is going—"

"Yes, they are. They're all going to be talking about me."

"Mom, not everyone is going—"

"They're all going to know my daughter hates me!"

"I don't hate you."

"Yes, you do. 'My mother committed serial marriage'? Any daughter who would write such a thing about her mother *has* to hate her. She *has* to. I didn't plan to be married seven times. It just happened!"

"Mom, I really don't think I—"

"Even my attorney and priest looked at the blog and asked, 'What is this thing? What is it? What has your daughter done?' This could entirely destroy my court case!" Mom had filed a lawsuit involving the dissolution and distribution of Vance's financial trust. If she won the case, she'd avoid dealing with his children for the rest of her life.

"Jesus, Mom. Why in the world would the attorneys care about this?"

"Because it's going to be part of my character assassination. And I guarantee you the other side already knows what you've said about me."

"You think their attorneys read my blog? You think people are automatically found guilty based on blog posts someone writes about them? Jesus, we'd all be in jail," I said.

"Oh, listen to you, talkin' like *you're* a lawyer or something."

I sighed.

"You know, you're a tough one," she said. "You act as if nothin's wrong, then you go and do somethin' like this."

"Mom—"

"I have to go," she said. "I have an appointment with my priest, who's gonna help me decide what to do about this."

"Oh," I said. "Yeah, okay."

"Satan is trying to destroy my marriage!" she said and hung up.

Her question was a valid one. What kind of daughter does such a thing to her mother? My kind.

She maintained radio silence for several days after our phone confrontation. For all I knew, her priest had convinced her to sever ties. A sick foreboding came over me when I saw an email from her pop up on my computer screen. She'd left the subject line blank. My hand shook as I clicked the mouse to open the message.

"Having a dinner party tonight."

She described the menu and how many people she'd invited. I responded with interest in her plans. Subsequent emails in the months that followed talked of recipes, weather, gardening, and our dogs. We never discussed the blog.

The last time I'd seen Dave, he'd once again been drinking heavily and had even shown up at the dinner table with a bloody gash on his nose, an injury he didn't remember sustaining. He filed for divorce, claiming Mom prevented him from seeing his children. Nothing could have been further from the truth. It was

Dave who so often complained about his children, ranting that they were all about money—the rattlesnake in particular, always begging him to bail her out of one financial crisis after another.

I'd never seen Mom so devastated, and she sent frequent emails telling me of her tears, confusion, and fear of the future. She also sent messages to me in the middle of the night when she found herself sleepless and scared. I'd become her confidante again. I constantly reassured her she would be fine and reminded her of the countless friends and family she had who always rallied behind her. The settlement negotiations began, and Mom said they went quickly and without much argument. Then she disappeared on me. After hearing nothing from her for weeks, I received an email from her: "I really need to talk to you."

"Then talk to me," I wrote.

"Will call you," she replied.

Her phone call came a few days later. "Are you sitting down?" she asked.

Chapter Twenty-Seven

Oddly, the day of her visit with William—her eighth marriage—she made no comment about our home or the way we'd decorated it. For once, I hadn't bothered to maniacally clean before her arrival and felt comfortable with the amount of dust coating every surface. I provided a silent and private tour as I opened the front door and led them out to the side deck.

This is my house and my dust. Smells a bit doggy in here, I bet. And yes, that's my cluttered kitchen over there with the dishes in the sink. And here we walk by the utility room, stuffed with dog towels, hair-filled dog beds with two napping blind dogs in them, bird suet cakes, vacuum cleaner attachments, and probably the smell of pet urine on the floor, but I don't smell it, and that's what matters. There's my wonderful husband out there on the deck, waiting for you, hoping you'll say you love our little cabin in the woods. It's the same man you did not like all those years ago. Let's go outside and sit around the patio table he wiped clean of pollen for your visit. Oh, you brought wine. I'll open it for you.

It's my house, and everywhere I look I see the consequences of my choices, and they're all mine, and that truth feels so damned liberating right now, I can barely stand it.

The four of us had a relaxed, easy conversation. I didn't talk much, didn't try to be funny, and didn't try to impress her. As I watched and listened that afternoon on the porch, I sat back and tried to picture her as maybe a neighbor of mine or a familiar face I often saw in town, though knowing the mental gymnastics required to make her no longer my mother were impossible to fully execute. She looked older and had put on weight, but the tiny muffin tops at the waistband of her jeans were endearingly cute. She was pretty, engaging, calm, easy to be with, and surprisingly devoted to William. Finally, at the age of eighty, she appeared to have found a "heart connection."

It took me fifty years to realize she and I are separate people. Her devastation at the discovery of my blog left me feeling gutted with a literal physical pain, as if I'd brutally severed our connection with a knife. I hadn't wanted severance—I hadn't intended it—and knowing I'd caused her such intense anger and hurt threw me into a tailspin of tears and sleeplessness for days. But when I began to allow myself to feel and truly investigate my own intense anger and pain, she could not help but sense the change in me.

For most of my life, I'd sought nurturing, assurance, protection, affection, and encouraging words from her, believing mothers have loving actions toward their children hardwired into them, which then carry over even when their children move into adulthood.

"Your mother loves you as much as she can," my childhood therapist had said. To me, it meant she held part of herself back from me, reserving it for someone more worthy. I worked for decades to earn her love in full and searched for available access to her emotionally. Maybe it could be obtained from accomplishing more, in being agreeable and easy-going around her, or through being less of a worry to her than my brother. Such behavior might have protected my status as her trusted little accomplice for life. If I behaved as someone other than myself, it might gain entrance to that off-limits space in her heart. We most likely could have continued in this manner indefinitely.

But when I quit drinking for several months after her discovery of my blog, I finally gave myself permission to stop banging my head against the wall of artifice, to stop behaving in ways not at all in keeping with my nature. I began to release unrealistic expectations of behavior in others and saw with clearer and sober eyes *what is*. When I stopped medicating the dysfunction, my relationship with Mom had no choice but to reveal what it was at its core. Remove an addiction, and good god, you'll find a hot mess hiding under it.

Then, damn if it sure didn't feel good. Like the day when you casually look around your house and note with genuine alarm, "This place is filthy! Someone oughta clean this up." And then it dawns on you: you're not only responsible for the filth, but you're that someone who needs to get off her ass and get busy cleaning. And then your house is set in a semblance of order, and you wonder how the hell you ever lived any other way.

Over the past several years I've spent countless hours trying to put myself in Mom's shoes to better understand her choices. I see photos of her at a certain time in her life and try to recall my emotional maturity at the same age, and this has contributed to my cutting her some slack based on age and/or inexperience. But then I see Dan's face a foot away from my tiny naked body, his fingers probing me, and see Mom doing nothing to protect me. I hear him repeatedly beating Greyson with a belt and see Mom doing nothing to protect him. Even worse than nothing . . . all those years, she pretended not to know.

And that's where the gentle understanding of her actions comes to a jarring, screeching halt.

Mom and William got up to leave a few hours later. He put his arms around me to hug me goodbye. "Your mother really does love you," he whispered in my ear.

I pulled back and looked into his eyes, confused as to why he felt the need to say this. My first thought was that Mom put him up to it. For the next few days, I attempted to parse any emphasis he might have placed on the words. Was it "Your mother really *does* love you." Or maybe "Your mother really does *love* you."

A few months later, my phone rang as I stood at the stove fixing breakfast. One look at the wall clock told me it was not going to be good news. No one ever calls us at seven thirty in the morning. "Honey, I got a few things to tell ya," William said. "Your mother's had a stroke."

The first stroke she'd had several years ago left part of her foot, and one finger on her hand, slightly numb. This second stroke affected the language center of her brain. She was released from the hospital after only a few days. Tests showed it was a serious stroke, but William could give me no details on exactly where in her brain it had occurred or what the doctors foresaw as the odds for substantial recovery. She could no longer email, and texting was easier for her than talking on the telephone. The day before I left to see her, she sent a message:

"Happy for u love" (heart emoji)

"Se u tomorrow" (heart emoji, heart emoji)

And she texted during my drive, although I didn't get the message until later that day:

"Waiting for you" (heart emoji)

"Us out."

"Hope all is going good for uou headed to us" (heart emoji)

"An you give us where you are."

I honked when I drove up their driveway and rolled down my window when the front door opened immediately. Mom came out first, followed by William. She wore what looked to be an expensive red-and-blue Chanel knit sweater and had coordinated it with little gray sweatpants. "Hey, Mom! You wore your best sweatpants for me!" I called out.

"Walmart," she said.

"She's just been frettin' and frettin' for hours, sure somethin' happened to you. She called and called," William said.

"I wasn't getting cell reception up here," I said over Mom's shoulder. She'd stuck her entire upper body into the car and was hugging me.

The next few hours involved me pulling out the gifts I'd brought, her showing me the house and feeding me pimento cheese and crackers, us walking the two dogs together, and then us driving in the steady rain in the dark to get to a restaurant. Our waiter was so indulgent and patient with Mom, I could have hugged him. She tried to explain to him that she couldn't talk well. "I had a . . . ," she said, rubbing her thumb and forefinger back and forth on her forehead.

"That means stroke," I told him.

She turned page after page of the menu as he told us about the specials. "I had something green last time," she said.

"Mmmmm . . . something green," the waiter said.

"Salad, maybe?" I suggested.

"Or was it a soup you liked, honey?" William said.

Some sentences she formed sounded perfectly normal, while she struggled to find words for others. "It was green. William, help me. I ate something green! Shit!"

"Now, honey . . ."

Somehow, we figured out that she'd had guacamole before. While we waited for the food to arrive, a steady stream of people came over to the table. "I had a . . . ," she said, rubbing her forehead. "What am I trying to say?"

"Stroke," I told them.

The group of four talked to her for about ten minutes. Then a young woman—a local dog groomer—from another table came over to talk to her. "I don't know if you remember me, but I just wanted to say hi."

Just as we'd get some momentum going in our conversation, someone else would drop by the table to say hello. William said it had been the same at the hospital. "We could barely even eat a meal," he said. I feared the same. "People were coming in and out of her room all day wanting to talk to her. She didn't need to be forced to talk, she needed time to heal."

I wondered why, then, he hadn't taken the bull by the horns and put a stop to it. But that night in the restaurant, I was reminded of how many people knew her. And more than that, I was reminded of how everyone seemed to love her. I took hold of her hand. "Still so pretty," she said, turning mine over in hers. She'd always loved my hands.

Mom and I held hands, and William and I had a grasp of each other's forearm. When he wanted to stress a point he was making, he'd squeeze or give a small tug at my arm. We must have looked like a particularly clingy family.

I learned that the stroke had destroyed much of Mom's conversational filter. If a thought came to her head and she was able to express it, she put it right out there. "William gets to see his family," Mom said, looking at him angrily. "I never get to see mine."

"Well, now that I see how easy it is to get here, I'll be able to visit more often," I said. She took on a vacant expression as she searched my eyes, and I wondered if she could tell I wasn't being truthful. It had been, in fact, quite difficult to make the visit happen.

When we got home, I called it a day quickly and ended up in bed with a book. Mom stopped in and stretched out on the foot of the bed. I asked what she'd heard about Greyson, who was in the process of buying a house. "Who's Greyson?" she asked.

"Your son. Greyson."

Her expression never revealed if such information truly registered, and she continued with her newly acquired free-association way of communicating. "William and I have to go to a big wedding next month," she said. "I hate this shit." She got up from the bed, asked if I needed anything, then headed for the hallway. "I love you!" she called out as she reached the staircase.

"Love you too, Mom."

"I love you!" she said, louder this time. I could hear the smile around the words as she said them.

The next morning, I was up, showered, and dressed by six. William, a kindred early-bird spirit, was already seated on the couch, reading a Christian devotional.

He'd made coffee. *Thank ya, Jesus.* I poured a cup, then sat down in a nearby chair. "I'm sorry if I'm interrupting," I said, pointing to his open Bible.

"You're not botherin' me, honey. I finished all I needed to this morning," he said, putting the material on the table beside him.

Mom had trouble sleeping ever since the stroke and lay awake for hours in the middle of the night, then slept late in the mornings. There was little for William and me to do but wait for her to wake. When she'd finally come strolling into the room every morning, his eyes would light up. "There's my beautiful girl!" he'd say. He poured more coffee for himself, then came back to the couch. "Your mother got out of bed this morning around three. She heard you moving around downstairs and was worried you might need something."

"I got up to go to the bathroom, that's all."

"She just seems to worry about you so much. She called and called yesterday, wanting to make sure you were on your way and safe. She kept going to the front door to watch for you. She couldn't concentrate on anything else."

I'm not at all into interaction first thing in the morning, not until I've finished a huge cup of coffee. The conversation was veering into dangerously weighty territory.

"You know, your mother doesn't feel like she was a good mother. This plagues her."

Oh, Christ. So, my mother worried about my safety, didn't want me to lack for anything, and beat herself up for a history of poor mothering. Good god, this was a lot to process. The sun wasn't even up yet.

Over the next few days, I found myself wanting to protect her. She didn't enjoy the prospect of conversation with others; finding the words she wanted to say proved too stressful.

"My brain," she'd say.

I wanted people to leave her alone, to stop making things so hard on her. I wanted her to myself. Few people called the house; I assumed William enforced this to further protect her from continued frustration. I'd never seen a man so in love with her. In the three days I was in their home, he never once showed impatience with her, even though she frequently took her frustration out on him. If he took a while to tell a story, she might even cut him off. "Now, do *I* get to say what *I* wanted to say?" she'd ask. At times it seemed as if she had been replaced by a new model. Truth be told, I genuinely enjoyed the New Filterless Mom.

The next morning, William and I had coffee at the kitchen table while we waited for her to wake. Whenever he and I were alone together, he talked of how much he adored her, and his eyes rarely failed to well up with tears. "I've just never felt such love," he said.

It was beginning to get old. Story after story about Mom and what a blessing from heaven she was, then he would tell the same stories again the next day. It seemed everyone who knew Mom viewed her as perfection. Over the years, I'd nodded and smiled and agreed when told what a talented and beautiful woman she was and how wonderful it must be to have her as my mother.

I used to believe in her perfection—had even put her on a pedestal for a time—and saw my growing anger and resentment over the years as a fault in my character. If she was perfect, the emotional chasm between us had to be caused by me, I reasoned. I'd grown prickly, cautious, and self-protective around this perfect woman. Up until the last several years, I was always too close to situations—dare I say enmeshed—to accurately dissect the dynamics of our relationship.

But this is yet another area in which I give William a tremendous amount of credit. He was willing to view me as a person fully entitled to my own feelings regarding my experience with her—sixty years of history he had flat-out missed, quite frankly, and he never assumed any right to find fault with how that history should now manifest itself within me. "Your mother had a lot of bad experiences when it came to men. And yes, a lot of it was her fault," he told me. "She doesn't feel she was a good mother."

Okay. Wow. But why did he feel the need to tell me this again? I dropped my head back, stared at the ceiling, and rolled my eyes. "Let's just say, it was *so* chaotic," I said.

"I think I can understand that," he said.

I again wondered if Mom had put him up to discussing her mothering. Given the challenges she now had in communication, however, this didn't seem to fit. But if her failings in this area had plagued her so, she certainly never let on. Now it was too late. Post-stroke, there seemed no way she and I would ever be able to work this out in words. Certainly not in words.

I told Mom the reason I'd slept so well at her house was because she came downstairs each night to tuck me in. She did no such thing, really; we just chatted in my room before she went up to bed. But I reminded her at the end of each day, and she would smile. "Don't forget to come tuck me in, okay?"

The night before I left for home, she came down to the guest room and stretched out at the foot of my bed. It was dark and windy with sleet on the way, and the forecast predicted a freeze around three in the morning. While some people seem to take comfort in storms, and even enjoy them, dark and rainy nights make me feel particularly threatened, and they at times even set off a deep sense of loneliness. "Mom, what is that?" I asked, pointing.

"What?"

"There's a light out there. It's moving around."

"Where?" she asked.

"Come look."

We got up and went to the window. "See over there? About midway up the mountain. There's a light moving slowly to the side, like someone's out there walking with a lantern."

"Oh, I see it!" she said.

"Isn't that just wilderness?" I asked.

"Yes. I think so. I don't know."

"Are there any houses way over there?"

"Mmmm," she said.

We stood shoulder to shoulder and watched the small, far-away light moving around in pitch black. "I wonder what that could be," I said.

"What are they doing?" she asked.

"Surely no one's out camping in this storm," I said.

"Oh, no," she said. "They better not."

The light continued its odd movement. At times it would stop, seem to backtrack, then continue on its way. It disappeared a few times, then would reappear slightly farther across the mountain. "There it is. It's back!" I said.

I watched her track the light on the faraway hillside with

eyes that now looked different after the stroke. When her mind didn't have to struggle to speak or remember, their focus was softer, with a touch of vacancy. At times like this, when she attempted to understand a situation or event, they took on a sort of pinpoint intensity. I regretted making her worry, especially about something that didn't even involve us. "I hope it will be okay," she said.

I didn't know if she was talking about the carrier of the light or herself. *God, I hope so too.*

I tried to read after she went up to bed but couldn't stop crying. I was due to leave the next morning and felt the physical pull in my chest that leaving her had so often brought on in the past. Through the death of my father, several friends, and cherished animals, I have grown to understand the sensation that the heart can feel as if it literally hurts. Without fail, I used to cry when I said goodbye to Mom, while noting she never did. The tendency toward tears upon leaving her had ceased long ago—exactly when, I couldn't say—and I both resented and feared the renewed sense of vulnerability.

There is no doubt whatsoever that I will remember this night. A recurring image places me in this same room in the future. I will look out the same window into the kind of darkness that always unsettles me and feel I would give anything to have her standing there beside me again, both looking out together, both wondering about a light we will never identify, a light the stroke most likely caused her to forget as soon as she took her eyes off it. "I hope it will be okay," I will remember her saying. And I will not be here for a visit, I will be here for her funeral.

I am crying because sixty years have slipped by with an ever-present chasm between us. I remind myself now, and make a mental note to always remember, that I blocked off parts of my heart from her for my own protection and sanity. I vow to remember this in the future if guilt and regret threaten to creep in and crush me, for when she is gone, she will be gone forever. There will be no do-overs for us.

Do I forgive my mother? I've wondered about this hundreds of times. Nowhere have I found a personally satisfying definition of the word. Does forgiveness mean we move on and not let the past at all affect our future? Impossible. Our shared history could never be simply boxed up and stored away. There was never a time in my life when my mother did not somehow affect or influence me, and much of this was my fault. It took me far too long to realize I truly am separate from her. We continued our odd and dysfunctional dance around one another for decades. So . . . forgiveness? I still cannot answer. I know the stroke, however, has turned her into someone who can no longer hurt me. Or maybe the effects of our shared experience have turned me into someone she can no longer hurt. But this night tells me her death will hurt like nothing I've ever felt before.

The next morning, William and I are back at the kitchen table drinking coffee, waiting for Mom to wake. "If she were on her own, if she didn't have you . . . ," I began.

"She couldn't do it, honey. Not the way she is now. It's a plastic-in-the-oven and metal-in-the-microwave sort of problem. She left a stovetop burner on the other day. And she's not allowed to drive. She can barely read." His eyes welled up with tears. "And things frustrate her so."

"When the time comes, if she finds herself alone, would she want to stay in this house? In this town?" I asked.

"Well, not necessarily. There are a lot of people here who

would take care of her, though. But you know, honey. There's no place in the world your mother would rather be than with you."

For weeks, I couldn't stop thinking about his words. *There's no place in the world my mother would rather be than with me. No place in the world. With me.* I loved the sound of it.

I tried to picture our future relationship as portrayed in the television commercial I often see. I will come into our guest room—which will have become Mom's bedroom—every morning and throw open the curtains, allowing sunshine to flood the room and wake her. "How are you feeling today, Mom?" I'll ask. We'll spend our mornings seated at the breakfast nook table, drinking coffee and admiring the birds at the feeder outside the window. I will dutifully take her to doctor appointments and monitor her medication doses. We'll work jigsaw puzzles together, just like the daughter and mother do in the television ad about bladder incontinence. That mother wouldn't even *think* about peeing on the sheets at night. She doesn't dare make life messy in any way for her daughter.

But so what? What if she did? What's a little muss and fuss after all your mother did for you? Don't be an ungrateful bitch and warehouse her in a facility. No, no, no. Can't you finally find it in that cold, hard heart of yours to put your grievances behind you? I mean, it's not as if she ever locked you in a basement and starved you. I shared my conflicted emotions with Drake.

"Whoa, whoa, whoa, whoa there," he said. "If you're thinking about moving her in with us some day, you'd better think again."

I don't want her to be alone at night. I don't want her to accidentally overdose on her medications. I don't want her to be by herself when brought to tears of frustration because she can't follow a recipe. Or cry out to an empty house when she can't figure out how to write a check, or have no one nearby the day she discovers she can no longer play her piano. No, I do not like the idea of strangers taking care of my mother. I will always ensure that she is warm and clothed; has a roof over her head, excellent medical care, and access to her friends and family. My mother will never go hungry. But I also know my home is not the answer to her future predicaments.

I look back and see our family's flawed humanity with what I hope is mature and heightened clarity. Mom, too, was once a little girl, and although her mother worked so terribly hard to provide for her and Aunt Lu, she raised them with emotional neglect. Later, an angry Dan arrived, and his idea to whip tiny children with belts certainly didn't come to him from out of the blue. Vance was sexually abused as a child by a relative and was in his sixties when his mother first told him she loved him. Many in the long line of my subsequent stepfathers brought drug and/or alcohol problems with them. And my alcoholic in-laws subjected Kyle to a fear-filled and insecure childhood, thereby creating a fear-filled and insecure man. So many of us wasted decades, and even lifetimes, denying the existence of our inner demons, and the damage to others radiated outward like tendrils. Lots of flaws and mistakes. Lots of pain. I get it.

But when I was a child, someone needed to be an adult. I believe there are acts we commit or allow to happen for which we do not deserve forgiveness. And while I do feel compassion for her misfortune of having two strokes, I am not willing to give Mom a Get Out of Jail Free card out of pity or guilt. Yes, she is ill now, but it was not so long ago that she was not.

And if there is such a thing as heaven on earth, Drake and I managed to snag a piece, and we vow to protect it. We live in a log cabin in the woods with our seven dogs, three cats, twelve hens, four beehives, countless birds, and several deer that appear with their fawns every day, waiting for us to toss apples and carrots to them. Hummingbirds and butterflies appear every year, and the numerous songbird nests we placed around our home fill with eggs every spring. I'm learning forest farming and how to help save endangered plant species. Our garden is a certified botanical sanctuary. Drake and I regard our marriage as a sanctuary as well—consciously guarded and protected. We start every morning having coffee in bed, planning our day, or often just sitting quietly with one another. As much as is possible in life, we maintain a drama-free zone around ourselves. So, no, that morning in the kitchen with William, I did not offer, should the day come, to take Mom into my home. I no longer hold out hope that there is an untapped reserve of love and nurture to be found within her if only I will continue to seek it. A long, long time ago, admitting this might have hurt like hell, but I've reached a point of acceptance. I will not contort reality because it hurts my heart less to believe a lie. She showed me time and time again that there were in fact many other places she preferred to be rather than with me.

Although Mom repeatedly said "I love you" to me, the words began to sound perfunctory and now feel abrasive to my senses. Maybe she believes that the three words, if repeated often enough, might convince me that she does love me. Or maybe she believes that the three words, if repeated often enough, might convince her.

Afterword

I had no contact whatsoever with Dan after his phone call to me over fifteen years ago. Mom told him that day to never contact anyone in our family again, and to my knowledge he never did. Last I heard, he suffered from dementia and Parkinson's. He died in 2020. His obituary stressed over and over what a family man he was.

I am not in touch with any of my stepbrothers and sisters.

My brother, Greyson, remarried a few years ago and is blissfully happy.

Drake and I have been together for almost twenty years, and I would marry him all over again. Rain on our wedding day truly did turn out to be a blessing. Oh, and sex? More than I ever dreamed possible.

I find it striking that Mom, Greyson, and I all landed in healthy and loving relationships. Good god, what a bumpy ride.

Acknowledgments

My thanks to She Writes Press for this opportunity. You are an amazing group of women, and I knew I was in good hands through every step of the process.

A million thanks to Jill of Swenson Book Development, whose expertise and keen eye turned the manuscript into exactly what I wanted it to be. I am forever grateful for your time, patience, and insight.

About the Author

Sondra R. Brooks graduated from Interlochen Arts Academy as a ballet major, studied musical theatre at Carnegie Mellon University, and earned a Bachelor of Business Administration from University of Phoenix. She is a three-time award winner in the International Writers' Digest Competition for her memoir/essays "Vincent," "The Magic Tumor Theory," and "Jimmy." Brooks has served as judge in various writing competitions and is a member of Authors Guild of America, Story Circle Network, National Association of Memoir Writers, and North Carolina Writers Network. She lives in a log cabin in the woods with three cats and seven rescue dogs. Her husband of seventeen years considers himself to be a rescue as well. She enjoys cycling, beekeeping, forest farming, organic gardening, and caring for her botanical sanctuary. She presently makes her home in Pittsboro, North Carolina.

Looking for your next great read?

We can help!

Visit www.shewritespress.com/next-read
or scan the QR code below for a list
of our recommended titles.

She Writes Press is an award-winning
independent publishing company founded to
serve women writers everywhere.